Secrets to a Successful Startup

Also by Trevor Blake

Three Simple Steps: A Map to Success in Business and Life

Secrets
to a
Successful
Startup

A RECESSION-PROOF GUIDE TO
STARTING, SURVIVING & THRIVING
IN YOUR OWN VENTURE

TREVOR BLAKE

New World Library
Novato, California

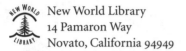

New World Library
14 Pamaron Way
Novato, California 94949

Text design by Tona Pearce Myers

Library of Congress Cataloging-in-Publication Data

Names: Blake, Trevor, author.
Title: Secrets to a successful startup : a recession-proof guide to starting, surviving & thriving in your own venture / Trevor Blake.
Description: Novato, California : New World Library, [2020] | Includes bibliographical references and index. | Summary: "A successful executive and serial entrepreneur examines why some startup companies succeed and others fail. Includes case studies, real-life anecdotes, and accessible explanations of basic corporate practices."--Provided by publisher.
Identifiers: LCCN 2019042403 (print) | LCCN 2019042404 (ebook) | ISBN 9781608686667 (paperback) | ISBN 9781608686674 (epub)
Subjects: LCSH: New business enterprises. | Success in business.
Classification: LCC HD62.5 .B554 2020   (print) | LCC HD62.5 (ebook) | DDC 658.1/1--dc23
LC record available at https://lccn.loc.gov/2019042403
LC ebook record available at https://lccn.loc.gov/2019042404

First printing, January 2020
ISBN 978-1-60868-666-7
Ebook ISBN 978-1-60868-667-4
Printed in the United States on 100% postconsumer-waste recycled paper

New World Library is proud to be a Gold Certified Environmentally Responsible Publisher. Publisher certification awarded by Green Press Initiative.

10   9   8   7   6   5   4   3   2   1

To Lyn and our many office companions:
Barnie, George, Freddie, Mabel, Albert, and Mavis.

And to startup entrepreneurs everywhere,
who are the lifeblood of any economy.

Contents

Introduction

Secrets to a Successful Startup is about how to conceive, plan, and launch your own business, one that is resilient enough to survive and thrive in today's marketplace. I am a serial entrepreneur, and I have built four successful businesses from scratch that have become $100-million entities. I have also written a previous guide, *Three Simple Steps*, about developing the right mentality to succeed in life. In this book, I focus on how to use that same mental approach to develop winning ideas and turn them into winning companies.

Globally every year, more than 50 million people start new companies, and the majority are single-person ventures like mine have been. Yet the failure rate of startups is shockingly, and unnecessarily, high. For every new startup, another established one fails. Of course, the reasons are varied, but I believe the most important are within your control. My hope is that *Secrets to a Successful Startup* will be the practical guide you need to help you succeed where so many others struggle and too often fail.

In my opinion, there is never a wrong time to start a company, and it is never too late to reinvent yourself. In 2017, 82 percent of new entrepreneurs were over forty years old, and 18 percent were over sixty. In addition, women owned 40 percent of all companies, up from just 4 percent in 1972. Since 2007, the number of women-owned businesses has surged 58 percent, while total businesses have only increased 12 percent. Further, technology has freed us from being slaves to a building. We can work from anywhere, even while traveling, and we can sell to anywhere and to anyone. In the United States, 69 percent of entrepreneurs start their businesses at home.

On its first day, a new startup can immediately attract a global customer base. There has never been a better or more exciting time to start a company, and achieving financial independence through your company has never been more attainable.

However, I have promised you secrets. Here are the first three. The first and most important ingredient for startup success isn't a talented team or the perfect product. It's not tons of cash, an eye-catching website, or a brilliant marketing strategy. It's you. Your mentality and approach, the way you think, make the crucial difference. If so many companies fail despite all the startup advisors, blogs, and courses, despite all the angel investors and MBAs, then there has to be something wrong with the way the majority of entrepreneurs think. Cultivating the right mindset is vital — both for coming up with a winning idea in the first place and then for building a winning company out of it — and that's the focus of part 1.

Here is the second secret: No matter what they're selling, where they are located, how big or small they are, or the state of the economy, the reason that most companies don't make it and go bankrupt is due to cash-flow problems. Entrepreneurs sometimes doom themselves right from the start because they don't structure their business, or manage their resources, in sustainable ways. Their expenses outpace income, they hire too many people, or they expand too fast. In part 2, I look at how to structure a business in order to survive the treacherous early days.

And the third secret? Be prepared to adapt. We live in the information age, when technology can change markets overnight. Yet most new startups, and many established companies, still commit all the sins of the bygone industrial age: They are too bloated, inflexible, and unskilled to react quickly enough. They stick to their well-thought-out business plan or to what worked yesterday — trying to sell what they want in the way that they expected — rather than adapting and changing to current market realities. In part 3, I explore marketing, sales, and how to build a trustworthy relationship with customers, along with what constitutes "the success mentality" — the collection of attitudes that startup entrepreneurs need to thrive and meet their customers' ever-evolving needs. This is the only way to survive long enough to hit a home run.

Leading expert Amar V. Bhidé, author of *The Origin and Evolution of New Businesses*, examined hundreds of successful ventures, and he concludes: "Coping with ambiguity and surprises is more important than foresight, deal making, or recruiting top-notch teams. Entrepreneurs don't need unique ideas and venture funding. Rather, they must be able to adapt quickly to changing business conditions."

Maybe that sounds radical, or more like common sense, but it's easy to forget and overlook, especially for eager entrepreneurs in the thick of starting their own company. That was me in 2002, when I came across a small book summarizing a Harvard study about why so many small businesses fail. The book highlighted a lot of reasonable advice — like the importance of knowing your industry, being able to identify the competition, doing what you love, and the value of being well capitalized. I devoured every word in the many case studies, but my firsthand experience was about to refute all the conclusions of those Harvard academics. I was about to discover that knowledge of your industry or even of your competition is not important because the day you start your company is the day it changes. I was also about to learn that companies don't succeed because you are doing what you love or even what you are good at. Yes, being well capitalized is essential, but the amount of money you start with doesn't make the defining difference, either.

A few weeks after I read the Harvard book, I had the privilege of meeting with George Rathmann, who *Forbes* magazine once called the "Bill Gates of biotechnology." Dr. Rathmann was chairman of a company called Ceptyr, and he wanted to hire me as VP of commercial development. I had already had my winning idea, but I was struggling to raise the necessary capital.

Over dinner, and purely out of curiosity, Rathmann asked about my company, and when I started to wax lyrical about my business plan and why its structure would give my startup a better chance of survival, he held up a hand to silence me. He said, "You do not know what business you are in until you get into the business. Just get started and adapt from there."

It is the best piece of business advice I have ever gotten. Soon after, we agreed to a mutually beneficial arrangement: I worked two days a week for Ceptyr, and for the other three days, I used the same office for free to execute my winning idea. Sadly, George Rathmann passed away in 2012 at the age of eighty-four, but I can hear his voice in my head every time I meet a potential entrepreneur wielding a hundred-page business plan.

The secret to success isn't in the plan. It's in the person holding it.

PART I

STARTING

The Global Pioneering Spirit

"Begin at the beginning," the King said, very gravely,
"and go on till you come to the end: then stop."
— LEWIS CARROLL, *Alice's Adventures in Wonderland*

Are you tempted to withdraw your savings, staple a resignation note to your boss's forehead, and walk away from the corporate world forever? Does the thought of never having to sit through another one of those dumb company meetings — you know the ones, where everything that can be said has been said, but not everyone around the table has said it yet — make you tizzy with excitement?

Or perhaps, have you been postponing your dream of starting your own business — maybe for decades as you focused on other priorities, like raising a family — and find that you don't want to postpone it any longer? Maybe the kids have flown the nest, you are at a loose end, and you desire to fulfill the potential you've always known you have.

If so, you are not alone. Every month in America, more than half a million people start a company, the majority being unregistered single-person ventures, with 69 percent of all startups beginning at home. In 2018, however, 670,000 new companies were registered in the United States alone. Women are majority owners of 40 percent of all the registered companies, but it is difficult to know the percentage of startups (various studies conclude between 25 and 45 percent). Further, according to a 2014 University of Phoenix Business School survey, some 39 percent of employees hope to own their own business. Contrary to what many in the media would have us believe, the statistics clearly show that the pioneer spirit in America is alive and well. These are happy statistics that fill us with hope for the American dream.

Or maybe running one's own business is a universal dream. According to research, more than 50 million new businesses are started globally every year. Of course, numbers per country vary widely and getting an accurate number is a bit of a lottery. Iceland was home to about 8,000 new businesses and India to about 85 million startups. Tel Aviv's startup ecosystem is one of the most highly developed in the world. Israel has more start-ups per capita than any other country, and its startups collectively raised $6.47 billion in 2018.

In 2017, the United Kingdom reached over 600,000 start-ups for the first time. London ranked as Europe's "most successful startup ecosystem," yet its output is half that of Silicon Valley. Meanwhile, startups in São Paulo, Brazil, create more local community jobs than Silicon Valley. Startups really are a global phenomenon, one fueled by modern communications technology, which allows anyone to start a company anywhere.

The one depressing statistic is that as many startups fail as start every year. Why? Lots of reasons. But mainly because entrepreneurs don't conceive of their startup in the right way or approach it with the correct mentality to begin with. Part 1 shows you how to avoid joining this negative statistic.

First, I explore where winning concepts come from and how to cultivate them. Then I look at how to turn that insight into a winning plan for a successful business.

CHAPTER ONE

Turn a Moment of Insight into a Winning Idea

A moment's insight is sometimes worth a life's experience.

— OLIVER WENDELL HOLMES SR.

When most people come up with an idea for a startup, they are inspired by something they do well, have experience with, or enjoy and are passionate about. In that moment, many startups are doomed.

My advice is: To come up with a winning idea, pay attention to what makes you mad. Don't focus on your skills or what you love and want to do; figure out what you want to change.

What Makes a Winning Idea?

When I decided it was time to be my own boss, I did what most people do. I considered what I enjoyed doing and what I was especially good at. However, when I analyzed my life honestly,

I had to admit that I was not very skilled at anything. It came as a bit of a shock to realize that I had no talent, but that revelation is probably what saved me from joining the millions of failed startups.

By my fortieth birthday, I had changed careers three times, and without much of a plan, I had become a sales manager for a biotechnology company. In essence, I was responsible for managing a sales team, which involved some skills, and I could lead a team, but those talents were not unique in any way. I could not figure out how to turn that experience into a winning idea for my own business. In addition, the dot-com bubble had already burst, I knew nothing about computers but how to type on them, and my lack of do-it-yourself skills was a subject of family legend. I had long been banned from going near a toolbox, so being any kind of tradesman was easily ruled out.

When I realized I wasn't getting anywhere struggling to solve this alone, I decided to research others who had faced this same problem. After all, this strategy had already worked for me once. When I was younger, I lived a hardscrabble life. I wanted to travel the world and to be an adventurer, but it seemed impossible. I couldn't work out how to escape the quicksand that was my life back then. So I read the biographies of explorers. Dozens of them had started out in even worse situations than mine, and their inspiring life stories helped me rewire my thinking. I began to mirror their attitudes and habits, and before long, I took my first adventure. Over the next two decades, my travels included lengthy visits to fifty-six countries.

Now I wanted to be my own boss, so I sought inspiration in the biographies of business pioneers. I hoped their inspiring stories would reveal some latent skill or knowledge that I shared with them. I wanted to know what talents had triggered their pioneering business journeys.

That is when the real "secret" to a winning idea hit me. It jumped right off the pages of every biography. It wasn't a particular talent or skill. It wasn't passion for what you are selling or doing what you love. It wasn't some innate quality that some entrepreneurs are born with. It wasn't some life experience or education that turned someone into a successful entrepreneur. In fact, the desire for success or to make millions seemed to be the wrong mindset entirely. Instead, the one thing every legendary entrepreneur had in common was that they were ordinary people who got so hopping mad about something they were driven to fix it.

Further, they did this even when they lacked the experience or qualifications to solve the problem. Most of them were clueless about where to begin. They didn't have top-notch management teams or access to funding, and in most cases they didn't desire to be entrepreneurs at all. They were simply driven by a deep motivation to find a way to fix something that had somehow got under their skin, and in the process they inadvertently became business leaders.

This is the simple yet profound secret to a winning idea: Be motivated to improve the world in one specific way.

Henry Ford grew up on a farm, and later he became an engineer working at the Edison Illuminating Company. He didn't set out to become an entrepreneur who would revolutionize the automobile industry and manufacturing. Instead, he was mad that, when he was growing up, driving a car was a rich man's privilege. Ford wanted to make cars that common folk could afford, freeing them to travel.

The story of Madam C. J. Walker is one of my favorites. The daughter of former slaves in the American South, Walker became angry because her hair kept falling out due to malnutrition, stress, and the damage caused by all the "snake oil" concoctions being sold by traveling salesmen at the end of the nineteenth century. She got so mad she developed her own hair tonic for herself. When other African American women began asking her for some, Walker started selling her hair tonic door to door.

By the time she died in 1919, Walker had become America's first female self-made millionaire and was considered the wealthiest African American businessperson, and she achieved this against almost unthinkable odds. She was the wrong color and the wrong sex in a racist, male-dominated society. She was the wrong class, she had no formal education, and she had no expertise in chemistry, beauty products, or business. Few successful entrepreneurs anywhere, at any time, have had as many hurdles to overcome, and I consider Walker one of my heroes. I wish I could have met her. If you could bottle what made Walker tick, you would surely make billions.

Another story that inspired me was Sir Richard Branson, whose dyslexia led to poor academic performance in school. His first business was a magazine called *Student*, through which he advertised discounted records for students, who typically couldn't afford the record prices at "High Street" stores. This made Branson mad, and he later said, "There is no point in starting your own business unless you do it out of a sense of frustration."

Selling records eventually led Branson to found a record label, Virgin Records. Then, another moment of frustration led him to start an airline. About thirty years ago, American Airlines canceled his flight to the British Virgin Islands, where "a beautiful woman" was waiting for him, and Branson became incensed.

"I went to the back of the airport, hired a plane, borrowed a blackboard, and wrote, 'Virgin Air, $39 single flight,'" he recalls. "I walked around all the stranded people and filled up the plane. As we landed, a passenger said to me: 'Virgin Airways isn't too bad — smarten up the service and you could be in business.'" Branson eventually married the beautiful woman, Joan, and turned his anger into a profitable airline.

Netflix cofounder Reed Hastings started Netflix after he was charged forty dollars in late return fees for a video at his local Blockbuster. "I had misplaced the cassette," he admits. "It was all my fault. I didn't want to tell my wife about it. And I said to myself, *I'm going to compromise the integrity of my marriage over a late fee?* Later, I realized my gym had a much better business model. You could pay thirty or forty dollars a month and work out as little or as much as you wanted." Hastings transformed his embarrassment and frustration into a new model for renting movies, and just as importantly, Netflix has since adapted with the times and become a global streaming sensation.

Sara Blakely was irritated by the seamed foot in her pantyhose, so she cut the toe section off. When she realized others had the same dilemma, she knew this common problem represented a business opportunity. Fearing ridicule, however, she didn't even share her business plan with her husband or family until her company, Spanx, was well underway.

Academics might try, but I can't find any genetic, psychological, cultural, or environmental commonalities between Ford, Walker, Branson, Hastings, and Blakely. Before starting their businesses, none had a shared identifiable talent or passion. What happened, however, what unites their stories, is that they used their experiences of frustration to do something to change and improve the world. That is where winning business ideas come from.

A Winning Idea Fills a Need or Fixes a Problem

However, the truth is, you don't necessarily have to get mad. But if your winning idea does not fill a need or fix a problem that frustrates customers, then it won't make a successful business, and by successful I mean one that makes millions by delighting those customers. Your business does not have to be the first to market to succeed. You don't have to be the only company offering your product or service. But you must fill a need or delight customers in a specific way and do that one thing better than anyone else (for more on this, see "What Makes a Winning Product or Service," pages 178–81).

For instance, Southwest Airlines was not the first airplane service, and within a year of their launch, with nothing much to distinguish it, the airline was in trouble. They had posted a net loss of $1.6 million, and the company was forced to sell one of its planes. Desperate to keep up, Southwest's vice president of ground operations, Bill Franklin, was tasked with finding a solution. The answer he came up with was simple but brilliant: Unload and load passengers faster than the other airlines, and get the planes right back in the air. So Southwest's "ten-minute turn," as it came to be called, was born, and they effectively turned the planes like an assembly line. This winning idea was born of adversity, but it worked because it served customers better.

The story of Google's founding is another tale of success born of frustration, but of a different kind. Two Stanford University doctoral students — Larry Page and Sergey Brin — had created a search engine algorithm (called PageRank), but according to Luis Mejia, Google's associate director of technology licensing, "The inventors did not want to do a startup company — they wanted to finish their PhDs." Mejia worked with the pair in the mid-1990s and says, "We spent half a year trying to market [the technology] and find licensees. But nobody really expressed much interest."

After a few "road shows," Mejia says, Page and Brin realized no one understood what they were doing. "So it was really out of frustration that they decided to start a company....In that respect, it was chance."

Mejia says the pair — who never finished their doctorates — did not have a business model, "but then a lot of things just sort of fell into place. Maybe that's where serendipity comes in....There is a chance we could have licensed it to another company for a very nominal sum of money. But it isn't clear that they would have done anything with it. And there probably would be no Google today."

Occasionally, moments of insight lead entrepreneurs to solve problems people haven't yet realized they have.

Ask Yourself: *What Makes Me Mad?*

Once I realized the "secret" to startup success, I reviewed my life for the things that made me mad. I drafted a long list, but one in particular made my blood boil. For years I had been frustrated that the company I worked for had created a product that could successfully treat a rare disease, but then they spent no money making physicians and patients aware that this solution existed. Though this sounds callous, it is typical of a lot of large businesses. Originally a small, private company that could make scientific and patient-focused decisions, it had become so successful that it went public. Now the company had to answer to shareholders, who generally prefer to increase profits and dividends and don't have much tolerance for potentially risky or low-revenue strategies.

The company estimated that less than two hundred people in the world suffered from this rare disease, and the cost of making all physicians aware of both the issue and the solution was considered exorbitant compared to the potential return from sales. Three times I proposed plans to justify an investment, and three times I was rejected and warned to focus on selling our other products. Yes, this made me mad.

My idea was born. I had never started a company before or raised finances, and I knew very little about research and development, but the unfairness of the situation motivated me to want to do something for patients suffering from the disease.

Take Notes: Make a List of Problems

Every time something gets under your skin, make a note of it. When you hear yourself or others complaining about something being wrong, jot it down. When someone expresses a wish for something that does not yet exist, scribble the request on a piece of paper.

Writing things down is important. Don't be fooled into thinking that making a mental note is all you need to do. It is scientifically proven that people who physically write something down tend toward taking action, and writing aids with memory retention. It is also scientifically proven that writing by hand creates greater retention than typing.

Good entrepreneurs keep a pen and paper handy at all times. This might be the simplest entrepreneurial tip of all: Never be without access to paper and pen, whether by the bed, in the kitchen, in the car, or in your pocket or purse. For the want of a pen, brilliant ideas have come and gone. Buy a stack of sticky notes and litter your life with them. I still do.

The first problem you identify may not lead to a winning business idea. Or the second, third, or fourth. Yet over time a pattern will emerge. Some things will make your blood boil more than others. In that pattern is the seed to a winning idea.

Find a Winning Solution:
Tap Your Intuition

Of course, identifying a problem is only half the battle. Discovering what makes you mad is only one side of the coin, and relatively speaking, it's easy. What's harder is coming up with an ideal solution, and what's harder still is turning that solution into a practical business. However, once you've identified something in the world you want to change, your next task is to figure out how to fix it. The winning idea is a problem-solution package.

Finding a winning solution requires accessing your intuition. This may not sound practical, but every successful entrepreneur I know does it. Analysis will only get you so far. Ultimately, you're seeking that famed lightning bolt of inspiration: the solution no one has thought of yet. People access their intuition in different ways, and some people are more comfortable with it than others. However, it's possible to cultivate your intuition in ways that invite inspiration, and I have developed tools that have helped me harness this power. While the process is still a wonderful, mysterious thing, the easiest and most effective ways I've found are through meditation and immersion in nature. Whatever methods you use, developing your intuition is essential for success in business.

The Power of the Feminine

In most cultures, intuition is considered a feminine trait. While it's something all people possess, women tend to be more open to it than men. Whatever the case is for you, the goal is to access and enhance your intuition so that it becomes a powerfully complementary, interconnected, and interdependent part of your intellect, or your ability to analyze, which tends to be considered a masculine trait.

I have been blessed in my life to be surrounded by determined women with powerful intuitions. I credit all my business success to the lessons they taught me when I was younger, even though they often had no idea I was paying attention. My wife, Lyn, is one of those women. Lyn "just knows." She is the only female in my soccer fantasy league, and she has won every year since she joined. I have come last on several occasions. Some of the participants spend hours studying form tables and injury lists. What they don't know is that my wife makes her predictions at the last minute and without any thought, and she still wins by a mile.

Lyn often ends her pronouncements with the phrase "I just know." Being male, it drives me to distraction. A typical conversation goes like this:

> **Me:** I'm going to invest in Bob's startup.
> **Lyn:** Don't, he's bad news.
> **Me:** How can you say that? You've never met him.
> **Lyn:** I just know.
> **Me:** How can you just know if you've never met him
> and have no idea what his business is?
> **Lyn:** I just do. It's up to you, but if you want my advice,
> I wouldn't do it.

Today, I take her advice, but it wasn't always that way. I had to learn the hard way. The first few times I ignored her intuition, it cost me, financially and mentally. Now I know better. I also know that my wife is not unusual. Many women have powerful intuitions, while many men ignore their own. Some people dismiss intuition because they think it isn't "logical," but that doesn't mean it isn't valid and real.

Who else trusts their intuition? Bill Gates. Steve Jobs believed intuition is "more powerful than intellect." Warren Buffett only makes decisions based on it. Richard Branson prefers it to "stats and data." Albert Einstein called it the "only real valuable thing." In a 2016 study, only one-third of the CEOs surveyed said they trusted their data and resulting analytics, while in another study, 59 percent of decision makers said that "the analysis they require relies primarily on human judgment rather than machine algorithms."

At Cornell University, Dr. Daryl Bem oversaw a decade-long series of experiments involving a thousand participants that showed humans do indeed have the ability to "sense" future outcomes. Because of the intuition study's paradigm-shifting implications, Dr. Bem waited until he had reached a "74 billion to 1" statistical certainty before releasing the results. By anyone's standards that is statistically significant. Dr. Bem said, "It violates our notion of how the physical world works. The phenomena of modern quantum physics are just as mind-boggling, but they are so technical that most nonphysicists don't know about them."

Yet the implications for business of embracing the power of the feminine goes beyond just intuition and coming up with winning ideas. This approach should inform how every business is run. For instance, one 2013 study concluded that women's abilities to make fair decisions when competing interests are at stake make them better corporate leaders. The study found that the more cooperative approach to decision-making translated into better performance for their companies. "We've known for some time that companies that have more women on their boards have better results," explained Professor Chris Bart. "Our findings show that having women on the board is no longer just the right thing but also the smart thing to do. Companies with few female directors may actually be short-changing their investors."

The researchers found that male directors preferred to make decisions using rules, regulations, and traditional ways of doing business. Female directors, in contrast, were less constrained by these parameters and more prepared to rock the boat.

Several other studies have shown that gender equity in senior management and at the board level brings many tangible benefits. In 2016, *Forbes* said, "Today's corporate world may be male-dominated but companies should take note: Hiring women is actually good for business. It's not just about equality, it's a business case with measurable success. Companies with more women onboard tend to outperform companies with more men onboard."

My own experience matches this data. While startups don't usually have to worry about hiring lots of employees or contractors and the composition of an executive board, it's a good lesson to remember. Strive for gender balance in hiring in the same way you strive to balance the feminine/masculine attributes in yourself.

Meditation: Training the Mind

Meditation is called mindfulness training because, like practicing a sport, it improves us in measurable ways and increases our mental and emotional skills through focus and repetition. If you want to improve your intuition, meditation is one of the best ways.

According to University of Iowa researchers, the brain's so-called "axis of intuition" is the ventromedial prefrontal cortex, which sits in the middle of the forehead. This is what gets depicted in cartoons of superheroes or spiritual gurus — a power emanating from the forehead. Further, a 2014 Wake Forest University study looked at the brains of fifteen volunteers before and after four days of mindfulness training. What did they find? In addition to a host of other wonderful brain enhancements, the freshly minted meditators seriously increased the "activity" and "interconnectivity" of their ventromedial prefrontal cortex. The ventromedial prefrontal cortex has been shown to play a key role in the extinction of conditioned fear responses and, importantly, in the maintenance of fear extinction over time. Fear is known to kill intuition.

Meditation can change your brain by eliminating fear for short periods, like thirty minutes, to create winning ideas and make better decisions. Every good idea I have ever had in business or life has come shortly after a session of meditation. I might feel fear before I sit in meditation — fear of problems, finances, growth, and so on — but by doing the meditation, I free my mind from fear and allow it to access solutions. It is the only method I know that helps.

There are many kinds of meditation techniques, and just like different forms of physical training in sports, they are used for different purposes and outcomes. Here, I offer one simple meditation technique that is intended to increase the frequency of great ideas.

Taking Quiet Time

I call this meditation technique "taking quiet time" (or TQT), and the whole thing takes about twenty minutes. It requires no skill or experience, and there are no advanced levels. It is a variation of a meditation technique that can be found in most spiritual practices.

The goal is to sit quietly, clear the mind, and for a few minutes think of nothing, which sounds simple but is actually very hard. It is contrary to the media-filled distractions of modern life and to how most of us have learned to behave. Yet to me, taking quiet time is the number-one business-growth tool in your arsenal.

Just like any sport, or any particular meditation technique, taking quiet time can be explained in simple or intricate terms, in four or four hundred steps. But if I want someone who has never played soccer to get excited about the sport, I will simply take them to a park and kick a ball around. If I first subjected the person to a step-by-step soccer lesson and explained every rule and technique, they would be bored to death. I want you to be excited about taking quiet time, so here is the four-step version. Kick it around for a while. If you want to know the intricacies of meditation, you can go as deep down that rabbit hole as you like (and a good place to start is my website, www.trevorgblake .com). But if you have never experienced the amazing benefits of meditation before, just try this simple process.

1. Get up thirty minutes earlier than your normal wake-up time.
2. Go to a quiet part of your home.
3. Sit upright in a chair, feet on the floor, hands over-lapped.
4. Do nothing for twenty minutes. Try to think of nothing. Focus on your gentle breathing through each inhalation and exhalation. When the mind chatter kicks in — as it always does, even for expert meditators — smile and imagine the words floating out a window. Then start again and focus on breathing.

That is all there is to it. I never time myself because somehow I always know when twenty minutes are up, but you might want to set a timer at first, in case you fall asleep — and there is nothing wrong with falling asleep.

Your Intuition Needs a Distracted Brain

Meditating and taking quiet time work in ways we don't fully understand. It seems counterintuitive that thinking of nothing could help improve intuition and inspiration, but it does. Not only that, it's been proven to aid concentration, creativity, self-confidence, problem-solving, analytical ability, and brain functioning.

The best way to find the brilliant solution we seek for our winning business idea is sometimes not to seek it. Instead, we consciously and deliberately empty ourselves of all distractions to make room for the kind of new inspiration that makes our stomachs flutter with excitement.

Why first thing in the morning? In a half-awake state, your brain is not as good at filtering out distractions and focusing on a particular task. It's also a lot less efficient at remembering connections between ideas or concepts. These are both good things when it comes to creative work, since this kind of work requires us to make new connections, to be open to new ideas, and to think in new ways. So, a tired, fuzzy brain is of much more use to us when working on creative projects like finding solutions to a winning idea.

In 2012, a *Scientific American* article described how distractions can actually be a good thing for creative thinking: Insight problems involve thinking outside the box. This is where susceptibility to "distraction" can be of benefit. At off-peak times, we are less focused, and we may consider a broader range of information. This wider scope gives us access to more alternatives and diverse interpretations, thus fostering innovation and insight. It is also noteworthy that when, for whatever reason, I skip my early-morning meditation session, sometime later that day Lyn will invariably say, "You didn't take quiet time today, did you?" When I don't, she says my self-confidence vibe is "off."

Connect to Nature: Expanding the Mind

As I read the biographies of successful businesspeople and entrepreneurs, another character trait that jumped out at me was their affiliation with nature. All of them turned to nature in times of stress or when big decisions needed to be made. Today, what I've found is that connecting to nature is a companion activity to meditation: It decreases stress, improves health, and sharpens the mind. To improve intuition and invite inspiration as you develop your winning business idea, take a walk in the woods.

This has been my approach in all of my businesses. I split my day up so that I have dedicated work times and dedicated distraction times. It is always when I close my office door and go for a thirty-minute walk in nature that the great ideas arrive. I notice, however, that if I skip my meditation in the morning, it doesn't matter how many nature walks I take. No great ideas come to me. The two are definitely bedfellows. Meditate, do some work, go for a walk: I've found this to be a pretty powerful prescription.

Henry Ford was passionate about walking in the country and reconnecting to nature. He encouraged workers to exercise in their off-hours and believed that, next to work, a person's duty was to think. Ford retreated to an old farmhouse near the family dairy in Dearborn. He sat on the ground when it was dry and in an old rocking chair when it was wet and simply let thoughts come to him.

Ralph Waldo Emerson was another who attributed his success, and his sense of tranquility, to being at one with nature. He spent as much time walking in a forest as working in an office because that is where he found his inspiration. Emerson described being in nature as "a high discourse; the voice of the speaker seems to breathe as much from the landscape as from his own breast; it is Nature communing with the seer."

To channel his restlessness, Cornelius Vanderbilt's mother paid him to clear and plant an eight-acre field. In that solitude, he came up with the ideas that made him a billionaire. I read that it worked for them, so I tried it and discovered that it worked for me. Kick it around. What do you have to lose? To enhance the benefits of taking quiet time, plug into nature and access its expanded reservoir of knowledge, just as a single computer plugs into the World Wide Web.

Here is my four-point nature prescription:

1. Reconnect with nature daily. No excuses. I consider this a necessity, as vital as eating, drinking, and working.

2. Keep reconnecting simple: Observe a flower and silently compliment it on its beauty, say hello to a bird, relocate an insect outdoors and wish it a safe journey, admire the landscape, stand barefoot on grass and experience the sheer joy of its coolness. You don't have to climb Mount Everest and sit on a pointy rock in a vow of silence. Nature *is* connectivity; being in it, you become part of its matrix. It will teach you. Just relax and listen.

3. Observe mostly in silence without doing anything else. If you take a stroll with someone and chat the whole time, you will miss the point and the benefit. I have lost count of the number of times I have seen dolphins or whales while the people around me miss them because they are gossiping, complaining, or exercising so intensely they aren't observing. Leave the phone behind; don't let calls or texts interrupt.

4. If you live in a concrete jungle, you may have to work harder to find nature, but she is all around: in the clouds, in window boxes, in grassy sidewalks. There is no difference or separation between a patch of grass in a disused parking lot and a giant oak in a wood. As Henry Miller said, "Even a blade of grass when given proper attention becomes an infinitely magnificent world in itself." All life is a doorway to reconnect with the force of nature. Go outside and observe, admire, respect. Simple.

Winning Ideas Create a Sense of Awe

A winning idea, when it comes, is not like a typical, everyday "good idea." Trust me, when you have a winning idea, you will know because you won't be able to stop smiling or pacing the kitchen floor. Meditation and connecting with nature are powerful ways to deepen intuition and expand connectivity into a universe of solutions. The flashes of insight we receive as a result are more like complete blueprints than "wouldn't it be cool" flights of fancy. They have us smacking our foreheads wondering why we never thought of them before, since they now seem so clear, so obvious, so perfect. Truly inspired, winning ideas induce a sense of wonder and awe.

That said, insights can take their own sweet time, and they usually arrive when we least expect them. Before I started my first company, I knew what made me mad. I knew what I wanted to fix. But I didn't know how. Every day for several weeks I meditated and connected with nature. Lots of ideas sparked in my mind, and I was careful to jot every one of them down. However, none of them were quite right. Then one day I took quiet time just before checking out of a hotel room.

An hour later, I was walking through a busy airport terminal when the solution to the problem came to me in a flash. It was not a vague idea or a notion. It wasn't a sketch. It was a detailed architectural blueprint, as if a diagram had unrolled on the floor in front of me. All at once, I saw the whole business model that could work to get those patients their medicine and make a profitable business. I actually stopped walking and let out a laugh that had other travelers thinking I had flipped out.

For my second company, the idea came to me while I was driving shortly after taking quiet time. I had to pull over and start writing feverishly on sticky notes. When I had it all written down, I continued driving to my appointment, but I could not get the idea to go away. So I canceled the appointment, turned the car around, drove home, and immediately set about turning the idea into a real company.

This is why you should never be more than an arm's length away from pen and paper.

How can you distinguish a garden-variety good idea from a genuine "winning idea"? What do awe and wonder feel like? In a way, it's like love. You know it when you feel it, and if you're unsure, you probably aren't feeling it. But I like how Emmy-nominated TV personality, filmmaker, and futurist Jason Silva puts it:

> It is an experience of such perceptual vastness you literally have to reconfigure your mental models of the world in order to assimilate it. One of the ways we elicit wonder is by scrambling the self so that the world can seep through. In doing so we feel such a blast of energy and expectation that we literally want to rocket to the moon. We feel stupefied amazement every time we think of our dream. It is rapture. It is magic. Only in these moments do we experience the power of a lightning strike in our minds and nerves. It is rhapsodic. It is what I saw in my wife's eyes every time we talked about it. She glowed. She floated. It was as if every time we talked about it, I had just placed a tiny puppy in her arms. That is awe. That is the state of ecstasy that must accompany a dream for it to have any hope of ever becoming reality.

Why is it so important to feel this strongly? First, it's how we identify a winning idea. But just as importantly, we need to be truly inspired by our dreams, since we will need that motivation to do all the hard work they require. According to one 2015 study, experiencing a sense of awe promotes altruism, loving-kindness, and magnanimous behavior. The researchers described awe as "that sense of wonder we feel in the presence of something vast that transcends our understanding of the world."

This is similar to the peak experiences described by Abraham Maslow, who wrote that these are "especially joyous and exciting moments in life, involving sudden feelings of intense happiness and well-being, wonder, and awe, and possibly also involving an awareness of transcendental unity or knowledge of higher truth (as though perceiving the world from an altered, and often vastly profound and awe-inspiring perspective)."

Thus, winning ideas inspire awe because they represent a profound desire to change the world in order to help others. They are solutions to problems that transcend ourselves. Yes, we may be happy for ourselves, too, but what really energizes us is feeling that larger sense of purpose, to be playing our part within the interconnected matrix of society and the world. Every time we think of our dream, we should want to dance on a mountaintop and scream with wonder and delight.

Enjoy the moment. Revel in it. Then immediately take steps to make that winning idea a reality.

CHAPTER TWO

Turn a Winning Idea into a Winning Company

Don't keep your dreams in your eyes, they may fall as tears.
Keep them in your heart so that every heartbeat
may remind you to convert them into reality.

— NISHAN PANWAR

When people have a winning idea and do nothing about it, the idea soon fades until it is forgotten. That is, until one day they encounter someone who has turned a very similar idea into a great company. Then there follows that sinking feeling in the pit of the stomach: That person could have been living a successful entrepreneurial life, if only…they had done something about their idea. What stopped them? Why didn't they follow through?

People talk themselves out of great business ideas all the time and for many reasons, but fear, negative thoughts, and a lack of self-confidence are the prime culprits. Like a kid touching a hot stove, people will convince themselves that any bad economic news, like a dip in the stock market, means that it's the wrong time to start a new business. But running a business is never risk-free, the economy will never be perfect, and waiting for the ideal conditions only risks letting your idea die from neglect.

Don't do that. Instead, immediately take action to make your business a reality, which builds momentum in the opposite direction. Once you discover your winning idea, incorporate it as a company. Online companies make the process simple and inexpensive (replacing the need for expensive attorney fees), and I consider this to be one of the simplest, least costly, and most effective things an entrepreneur can do. In fact, in 2018, according to the Small Business Administration, 70 percent of all businesses in the United States are sole proprietorships, and 99 percent never register their business, which is crazy given all the benefits. The legal protection alone is worth the small cost, but where it really pays off is psychologically and emotionally.

The benefit of reacting forward cannot be overstated. Once you incorporate your company, you have set your idea in motion. You have established a business, one that you own. You are the boss, and you have the paperwork to prove it. Doesn't that feel exciting? Doesn't that build self-confidence? Doesn't that add to awe?

Now every time you see the paperwork, you cannot help but plan the next step, which is figuring out all the nitty-gritty details for how you will accomplish the business you've just created (which I discuss in the next chapter).

The RAS Conundrum: We Focus on What's Urgent and Important for Survival

Every second, our brains are bombarded with about two million bits of data from our senses and nervous system. That's more information than we can process into conscious thoughts, and so our brains have developed a system for filtering and prioritizing information. If our brains didn't do this, our consciousness would be overwhelmed, and we'd be too overloaded to make decisions.

The part of the brain that handles this function is called the reticular activating system, or RAS. Psychologist Jerome Bruner said the "inhibitory system" of the RAS "routinely and automatically removes from perception, reason, and judgment over 99 percent of available fact."

Through various neural paths, the RAS connects the brain stem to the cerebral cortex. The brain stem controls many involuntary functions and bodily reflexes, while the cerebral cortex is believed to be the seat of consciousness and thinking abilities. The RAS links these two regions and helps our consciousness focus on what's most important or urgent in any particular moment according to the belief system we have developed since birth. This is essential, but it's also a double-edged sword.

Out of those 2 million bits of data we receive every second, we only have the capacity to process around 147 bits. Pause for a second to digest that. As Bruner said, our RAS filters out nearly everything we experience, more than 99.99 percent, and hides it from our awareness. This is a conundrum: In every moment, we are blissfully unaware of almost all of the world around us. The RAS filters out whatever we have decided, through learned beliefs or mental habit, is not important, and it allows into consciousness only whatever seems most relevant or needs immediate action. What does this mean for a first-time entrepreneur who wants to start a business? If we believe, for whatever reason, that it is the wrong time to start a company or that we lack the talent or ability to run a company, the RAS will let through information that supports these beliefs and filter out any contrary evidence. Any established negative habits or thought patterns will be reinforced, and in order to change them, we have to *decide* to change them and consciously choose to expose ourselves to new sources of data. In other words, we have to alert the RAS that it needs to focus on something new that's more urgent and important.

For instance, the RAS is the reason that, every time you learn a new word, you then start hearing it everywhere. It's why you can tune out a crowd full of talking people, yet immediately snap to attention when someone says your name. Advertising tries to hook the RAS: When you see a new car commercial that causes an emotional response, you tend to notice that car whenever you see it next.

Normally, all of this happens without us noticing. The RAS filters the world through the parameters we give it, which includes our philosophical, religious, and political beliefs, as well as our beliefs about ourselves. This helps to explain why we repeat negative behaviors even if they hurt us. If we expect failure, the RAS reinforces that by filtering out any contradictory information. On the other hand, if we feel empowered or expect success, the RAS will focus on data that confirms and supports this.

Because of the way the RAS functions, it's difficult to change repetitive or habitual thoughts, behaviors, and experiences. Yet it's possible by deliberately changing what we focus on. Bit by bit, we can reprogram our RAS and gradually change the world we experience. Instead of letting a winning idea fade, we deliberately feed the RAS a new goal by incorporating the idea immediately. This is not positive thinking. It's positive re-action, and that makes all the difference.

Positive Reaction:
The Psychological Benefits of Incorporation

Maybe the most important benefit of incorporating your winning idea is that it immediately starts to retrain your RAS.

Once you take action and make an emotional commitment to the idea, you are saying to your RAS: *I am serious, this is important, and I want this.* Obviously, your incorporated company will not have much substance to it yet and maybe not for a while. That is not important. What is important is that you are acting on your intentions. You are breathing life into your winning idea and taking the first tangible steps to creating your own business.

Below, I explain how to complete the process of incorporation online. Usually only a few days after you do so, the paperwork will arrive in the mail. If seeing your company name in a bold header, with your name and title as owner and CEO, doesn't give you a thrill and make your stomach flutter, maybe you shouldn't start a business after all. If it does, this will give you a massive emotional and psychological boost. Your RAS will shift gears and start gathering all the information it can to help you succeed, as if it were saying: *Hang on a minute. This is real. This is no longer just a crazy idea. Red alert. Time to reconfigure our pathways. Looking for complementary sensory data now!*

Continue to support this positive reinforcement in every way you can think of. Make copies of your incorporation papers, and populate your life with them. Keep copies on your desk, next to the bed, in your wallet, in the car, in front of the TV, and just about anywhere you spend time. Create letterhead and business cards with your company name (and a logo; see pages 215–16), and take them with you everywhere you go.

This is essential. Every time you notice these, it will make you think about your business, and each thought will inspire you further and retrain your RAS. The more you do this, the more you rewire your brain to a new way of thinking. The more you rewire the brain, the more attention you place on the company. And what we pay attention to...grows.

While you commute to work, as you think about the paperwork in your briefcase, you might start to imagine how your company will be structured, who will manufacture the product, and who the ideal customers will be. Your RAS takes all this on board, and before long your attention will be drawn to billboards, articles, and commercials that you somehow missed before but which now help you continue the process of reacting forward. This launches what feels like a magical process of serendipity, as things fall into place, but it is simply the power of your attention. Your RAS is helping change the 147 bits of data to include your successful company and filtering out the rest. It takes time, but it works...always.

Read the paperwork again before going to sleep, and your dreams might help you solve difficult problems, like how to raise finances and what the final product will look like. You might fantasize about the difference your company will make in the lives of others or even what it will feel like to sell the company for millions.

As you sit in yet another mind-numbing work meeting or are doing the laundry, sneak peeks at the incorporation paperwork. Every glance gives you a psychological boost, and every boost increases your level of self-confidence that you can make your company real. Every glance rewires your brain to a new way of thinking, builds momentum, and keeps you on the path to startup success.

The Positive Effects of Reacting Forward

I recently observed firsthand the practical effects when someone reacts forward and when they don't. During a remodeling job at my home, I was impressed by the quality of the work of the three-person team, but Anne stood out. She was the youngest and newest to the company, but she went the furthest to ensure that I was a satisfied customer. She seemed to be the main source of inspiration for the other two, and she was also the one who had the most innovative solutions to problems.

I asked her if she had ever thought about starting her own company. Her eyes lit up, and she confessed that she was always thinking about it. But just as quickly the light faded in her eyes, as she said she didn't think she could pursue her dream.

I pushed a little and asked what she had done to try, beyond just having an idea, and Anne reeled off a list of reasons why she had done nothing. She thought she did not have sufficient savings, and the economy was too shaky. She felt she might be too young and inexperienced. She lacked self-confidence, which wasn't surprising to me given the content of her thoughts. She was stuck in negative expectations, which reinforced themselves, since her RAS obediently identified all the reasons she couldn't start a company, rather than helping her solve the problem of starting one and taking the next step.

When I suggested that Anne incorporate her business and turn her idea into a real thing, her expression changed to confusion, then fear. This is a common enough reaction. To Anne, this sounded complicated and daunting. I explained it was neither of those things, and I described the positive psychological effects of reacting forward, but she didn't act on the advice. Even today, she still dreams of being her own boss but has yet to take action to start her own company.

Fred demonstrated the opposite reaction. He worked as a software engineer for a well-known company, and he was always coming up with interesting product ideas. Acting on my advice, he incorporated his best idea as a company, and every time he glanced at the corporate paperwork, he became more enthusiastic. He said to me, "I started to think that perhaps it was not such a crazy idea. At first, I tried to shake the idea out of my mind. Who was I to think I could run a company? Seeing the documents everywhere I went somehow made it seem less and less crazy, until I knew I had to do it. It got to the point where I knew I'd never be able to forgive myself if I didn't try to do something with it. I know if I had not made the idea into a legal company, and kept reading the paperwork, I never would have had the confidence to try it out."

Fred fleshed out a business plan during his spare time, and he asked one of his best clients for some feedback. Fred really just wanted reassurance, but the client loved the idea, and as chance would have it, he also had investor friends who were equally impressed. In the end, Fred was able to attract $5 million in investor funds, and he is now the CEO of his own company. When I saw him recently, his confidence astonished me. He still has no business training, but he rewired his way of thinking, and now he thinks and acts like a CEO.

This is what reacting forward can do: It builds the self-confidence to pursue our dreams. Once we take the first concrete steps down the path, and put ourselves in motion, it reinforces all the next steps we need to take.

Other Options for Reacting Forward

There can be other ways to move forward with your winning idea without incorporating. The simplest way is to just start conducting business. When you do that without incorporating, you are what's called a sole proprietorship, which is the simplest and most common business structure. This refers to a business owned and run by one individual with no legal distinction between the business and you, the owner. You are entitled to all profits and are responsible for all your business's debts, losses, and liabilities. You do not have to take any formal action to form a sole proprietorship. As long as you are the only owner, this status automatically comes from your business activities.

But like all businesses, you need to obtain the necessary licenses and permits, and regulations vary by industry, state, and locality.

A sole proprietorship, however, is legally vulnerable. As I discuss later, even sole proprietorships should take the step of incorporation, especially since the process is so simple and inexpensive.

You might also form a partnership agreement if you are going into business with one or more others, but again, this is risky without the legal protection afforded by incorporation. You will get some of the same psychological benefits by doing either of these, but I still always recommend that people incorporate their winning idea.

A winning idea is likely to require investors, manufacturers, suppliers, and other formally structured entities. These entities are typically incorporated businesses themselves, and for legal reasons, they can be restricted in working or contracting with unincorporated businesses.

The Practical Benefits of Incorporation

Still not convinced? Beyond the psychological benefits, how does incorporation help? Glad you asked.

As I say, when an idea is incorporated, it becomes its own legal business. This new business entity transforms the way the business is seen through the eyes of the law, and it often has more credibility with potential customers, vendors, employees, banks, and investors.

For instance, consider Google's cofounders, Larry Page and Sergey Brin. For two years they ran Google without incorporating, since they didn't see any need to and it was an expense they felt they could do without. Then one day Sun cofounder Andy Bechtolsheim decided he wanted to become an investor, but he wanted to invest in a company, not two guys. So

Bechtolsheim wrote a $100,000 check to Google Inc., an entity that did not then exist, and handed it to Page and Brin, who got the message. On September 4, 1999, they filed for incorporation in California as Google Inc., opened a bank account in the newly established company's name, and deposited Andy Bechtolsheim's check.

Andy Bechtolsheim wasn't teaching them a lesson in the power of reacting forward, since they were already working on the business. He was teaching them a lesson in common sense. With a sole proprietor or partnership, there is unlimited personal liability for business debts or lawsuits. That means if you went out of business, creditors could target your personal assets, such as your home or vehicle, as well as the personal assets of any investors who, by investing, become partners in the business. When you incorporate, you are responsible only for what you have invested in the corporation. That advantage alone is worth the few dollars it costs to incorporate.

Here are some other practical advantages to incorporation:

Legal Protection for a Purchaser

That asset protection is also important if you ever decide to sell your company. The purchaser of an incorporated business will not be personally liable if the seller did something unlawful, whereas if someone buys a sole proprietorship, they can be held liable for what happened in the past. Many successful small businesses are purchased by larger businesses, so the investment in the paperwork is essential to make that a smooth transaction.

Tax Savings

There are several tax advantages to incorporation. Your company becomes a distinct legal entity, even if it remains no more than just a file on your desk. That means that any business-related expenses, including some home-office operating costs, become tax deductible. Sole proprietors can deduct business-related expenses, too, but the benefit is often less. Sole proprietors report their business income on their own personal tax returns (Schedule C), and they also pay self-employment tax on the profit (Schedule SE), which at the time of writing is over 13 percent. In some cases, sole proprietors end up paying more in taxes due to self-employment taxes, and they are said to have some of the highest audit rates with the IRS.

Credibility

The abbreviation "Inc." or "LLC" after your company's name adds a touch of professionalism and credibility on any company stationery, especially with customers and lenders. Image is important, and customer confidence is tied to perceptions of your company.

The Simple Process of Incorporation

Incorporating a company is easy, takes only a few minutes, and costs less than a couple of hundred bucks. Costs and registration requirements can vary by state. However, dozens of online companies specialize in incorporation and have all this information, and the entire process can be completed by yourself online. Simply search in your browser "how to incorporate a company."

Be aware that some companies, particularly larger outfits that advertise regularly on TV, will sting you with add-on services and unnecessary monthly-maintenance fees. Their online narrative is also designed to make the process sound complicated and fill you with fear so that you will hand over a bigger check. Don't fall for this trick. Read the small print or avoid these firms. Seek out a company that makes the process transparent and effortless, since it absolutely should be.

Though filling out the forms is easy, incorporation does require you to make some initial, important decisions about your company. These require some advance consideration, which are as follows:

- Which state will you incorporate in?
- What is your company name?
- What type of corporation is it?
- Who is the registered agent?
- What are the articles of incorporation?

Which State Will You Incorporate In?

Most single-person corporations choose to incorporate in the state where the owner lives and works, and that's what I recommend except in a few rare cases.

One reason some people choose incorporation in a state other than the one they live in is because tax rates vary from state to state. Some states, like California and Hawaii, have tax rates around 10 percent. States like Florida, Nevada, and Washington currently have no state income tax, and that can be advantageous in certain situations, especially if you plan to sell your company at some point.

However, if you're operating your business in a different state, incorporating in a tax-free state won't excuse you from paying business taxes in your home state. Every state requires businesses operating within its borders to pay tax on sales or revenue that originates within the state.

Some large companies incorporate in other states that are

particularly pro-business, like Delaware. The Delaware General Corporation Law is considered one of the most advanced and flexible corporation statutes in the United States, and for that reason, over a million companies, including half of Fortune 500 firms, choose Delaware. However, if you are still at the stage of simply incorporating an idea, I recommend just using your home state.

What Is Your Company Name?

This is probably the hardest question to answer, since many people drive themselves crazy trying to come up with a catchy name for their company. Choosing your business name is obviously important, but it's less important than people think. In short, my advice is to spend no more than a few hours considering possible names, and do not pay good money to hire anyone to do this for you.

During the online incorporation process, the service will run a company name search to ensure that your choice is unique in your selected state, and then you register the name.

Here are my tips for naming your company:

- The more the name reflects your product or service, the easier it is for the customer to remember.
- Trust your instincts. If it feels right to you, go with it.
- If you're unsure, take a plain piece of paper and scrawl out a series of words and names, playing an association game. Keep going till certain words and ideas stand out. Go with it.

Don't stress about or get stuck trying to come up with a memorable company name. Remember: A successful product or service is what turns a company into a household name, and a great name can't hide a lousy product or poor service. Your winning idea is going to make or break your company, not what you call it. That said, if your business provides a service, the name should reflect that service, so it's easy for customers to remember when they need you.

For instance, who can deny that the name PayPal describes its service well? You might be surprised to learn, however, that the company was founded in 1998 as Field Link, and it was soon renamed Confinity. Only when Confinity was acquired by X.com and went public was the firm renamed PayPal. What about eBay, the company that acquired PayPal for $1.5 billion in stock in 2002? eBay was originally called AuctionWeb. Obviously, weak original names did not stop either company from succeeding.

Companies with great names like Circuit City fail as much as ones with nonsense names like Flooz.com, and yet nonsense names don't stand in the way of success, either. I have heard management consultants wax lyrical about the brilliance of the Amazon name, but founder Jeff Bezos actually came up with it on the fly. He wanted a name that was at the head of the alphabet, so it would show up first on list services when he started as an internet book retailer.

Many successful companies change their names over time as their businesses evolve. For instance, Google was originally called BackRub. Then a year later, after a simple brainstorming exercise between the two founders, they changed the name to Google. Even Microsoft started out as two words, Micro and Soft.

In the end, choose a name that works right now. If you decide to change the name, it's easy to do and does not cost anything. You do not have to go through another incorporation process. You simply update the information online through the state website where you are registered.

What Type of Corporation Is It?

Like choosing a company name, choosing a corporate structure can seem daunting and intimidating. Every type carries different tax implications, has different rules, and can be preferred depending on your situation. However, for individuals who intend to own and run their own business, with no or few other employees, there is really only one structure I recommend: a limited liability company (LLC).

In the United States, LLC registrations outpace other corporate structures. For their simplicity alone, they suit most entrepreneurs' startup needs. In 2017, according to the National Small Business Association, the majority of small businesses it surveyed are LLCs (35 percent), followed by S corporations (33 percent), corporations (19 percent), sole proprietorships (12 percent registered, most unregistered), and partnerships (2 percent).

In addition, just like your company name, you can alter your company structure at a later date if it makes sense as your company expands.

If you're unsure what's best or how incorporation will affect your taxes, consult with an accountant or other financial professional. And remember: Whatever decision you make doesn't have to be permanent. You can switch from one business structure to another (though it does require more paperwork and more fees). Here is a quick overview of US corporate structures:

General Corporation

Also known as a "C" corporation, this structure allows as many shareholders as you want and is more typical of large public companies. If your company is in an industry that typically needs a lot of startup capital, like tech firms often do, or if you have aspirations of eventually holding an IPO, then a C corporation might be a better choice.

The problem with the C corporation is double taxation, since it is taxed at both the federal and state levels. Profit distributions are also taxed at the federal and state levels. If you are planning a small business with at most one or two other partners or investors, then avoid this structure.

Close Corporation

Shareholders are limited in number to thirty. Not all states recognize close corporations, so most small businesses choose an alternative structure.

Subchapter S Corporation

An "S" corporation is a type of general corporation that has a special tax status with the IRS that permits business owners and entrepreneurs to be taxed as if they were sole proprietors. S corporations avoid the double taxation of a general corporation, but there are some restrictions to ownership. Only citizens or permanent residents of the United States can be involved, and the shareholder limit is set at seventy-five. For single-person and small businesses, other restrictions make it a complicated structure that can be distracting when someone is starting as a sole owner.

Limited Liability Company

This structure provides the limited liability protection of a corporation with the "pass through" taxation of a sole proprietorship (all revenue and expenses pass through the business to become the owner's personal income). Also, members of an LLC are able to divide company profits in any manner, regardless of ownership in the company. This flexibility allows an LLC to allocate profits and losses to the greatest tax benefit of the company's members. Every state recognizes the structure, and there is greater flexibility in how they can be organized and managed.

Limited liability companies can usually sell "stakes" in the business, which act a lot like the standard shares of a corporation. The difference is that anyone who buys a stake, no matter how small, will have as much decision-making power as any other member of the LLC.

Certain types of businesses that provide professional services requiring a state professional license, such as legal or medical services, may not form an LLC, but they use a very similar form called a professional limited liability company (PLLC). In Europe and Asia the LLC structure is replaced by the Limited (Ltd.) entity. They are not exactly the same, but the liability of members or subscribers of the company is limited to what they have invested or guaranteed to the company.

Who Is the Registered Agent?

You are required to name a "registered agent" in the state of incorporation. A registered agent is simply someone who is available during normal business hours to receive legal and tax mail for the company. Designate yourself as the registered agent because you are the one who collects the mail. Most online companies do not explain this, and they can trick you into paying unnecessary fees to act as the registered agent for your company.

What Are the Articles of Incorporation?

All new LLCs must file articles of incorporation, which are also called "articles of organization," with their secretary of state's office. That sounds intimidating, but it is just a short form that records the names of the LLC and its members, along with their contact information. A single-person entity has one member who is also a manager, and that person becomes known as a member-manager.

Although this is often not required by law, you will be offered the chance to draft an operating agreement for your LLC that spells out the details of the business arrangement, including percentage ownership for you and any other shareholders, along with roles, rights, and responsibilities. For most single-person companies, you simply assign 100 percent of the share of ownership to yourself. If others are involved, the online form isn't much more complicated than filling in their names and mailing addresses.

CHAPTER THREE

Make That Company Real

Draft a Winning Business Plan

By failing to prepare, you are preparing to fail.
— often attributed to BENJAMIN FRANKLIN

Once you've incorporated your winning idea, the next step is to create a business plan. Most entrepreneurs want to avoid or skip this, particularly if they aren't trying to attract investors. However, no matter what your business, I think creating a business plan is the best way to start. Not producing a business plan is like trying to build a car from scratch without any instructions. The process of drafting the plan is the way you figure out how to build and run your company. Further, it's the way you test-drive that car to see whether it works before you risk taking it out into the real world.

I have gone through the business-plan process for each of my four companies. For two of them I went through the process again during their growth stages. In each case I produced a lengthy document that served as my bible when any vendors or investors asked me any questions, and I always sounded like a confident and knowledgeable entrepreneur on conference calls while my fingers did the walking through the pages. But no one has ever asked me for a copy of a completed business plan. This supports my theory that the primary purpose of the process is to benefit you, the entrepreneur.

Discussing the business-plan process means getting into the minutia of markets, business functions, and financials. Personally, I think reading about business plans can be a bit boring, but I can assure you that the process itself is not. Ultimately, success isn't measured by the document you produce but by what you as a business owner learn about your market, the customers, and the competition.

Another reason for going through this process is to help attract investors and your preferred vendors. For investors, your plan needs to include an executive summary, from which you develop an elevator pitch, and we'll look at those in detail. If you are self-funding, you don't need those. For vendors, you need to focus on and share the specific sections relevant to their service, whether that's manufacturing, financial forecasts, or marketing.

Invariably, during the process, you will discover unexpected problems and opportunities, and you may need to adjust and adapt your plan, product, or service accordingly. Basically, that is the main point of doing this in the first place. Even if no one else reads the plan, this ensures that your business will fix what you want to change and do so in a way that supports a successful business.

Finally, through this process of discovery and decision-making, you will continue to rewire your brain and build self-confidence and expertise. You will acquire deep insight into your prospective customers and the market, and you will continue building positive psychological momentum. By the time you finish the process, you will be itching to get started as your own boss.

Yet despite the evidence for the importance of completing a business plan, one study by *Inc.* magazine found that only 40 percent of the founders of companies on its top-500 list had bothered to write a formal business plan. Only 12 percent said that they had conducted formal market research before launching their enterprise. Is it any wonder that so many start-ups fail?

There are no shortcuts to success.

A Business Plan Is a Process That Cultivates Success

To me, what's most important about a business plan isn't the final document. It is the process. The process of investigating your business, your customers, and your market is another form of reacting forward. In the end, your winning idea, as originally conceived, may not make the ideal business, but through this process you will learn what *does* and *will* make a successful business and how to see it through.

Research and experience back me up. A producer of business-plan software conducted a survey that found that those who complete business plans are nearly twice as likely to successfully grow their businesses as those who don't write a plan. Regardless of the type of company, the growth stage, or the person's intention for the business plan, the study found that writing one correlates with increased success in every business goal the study identified. These included obtaining a loan, getting investment capital, making a major purchase, recruiting a new team member, thinking more strategically, and growing the company.

The authors concluded: "While our analysis cannot say

that completing a business plan will lead to success, it does indicate that the type of entrepreneur who completes a business plan is also more likely to run a successful business."

This raises an interesting question: Are the people who are most likely to succeed anyway the ones who usually create business plans, or does drafting a plan help teach and instill the behaviors of a successful entrepreneur? I think it's both.

One way we learn is through imitation, and this is hardwired in the brain. In the early 1990s, a team of Italian researchers discovered individual neurons in the brains of macaque monkeys that fired both when monkeys grabbed an object and when monkeys watched another primate grab the same object. This led to the discovery of what are called *mirror neurons*, which allow animals to observe and mentally mimic the actions and feelings of others. This is how we learn from others without necessarily going through the same experience. For instance, if someone stubs a toe on a raised paving slab and winces in pain, we grimace with empathy, since we mentally re-create what they are going through. Later, this helps us remember to step over that stone so we do not suffer the same injury.

This is analogous to what startup entrepreneurs do as they create their business plan. They are trying to identify and avoid the mistakes of others in the same industry while also identifying and mirroring the best practices of those successful companies that are doing it right.

Further, this process of discovery fosters the right attitude to achieve success. The more data we collect, the more we understand, and this reduces fear and anxiety and increases feelings of competence. This creates a sense of flow, which is a sense of happiness and achievement right now as we work toward future goals. This relates to a concept called the "paradox of intention," which states that we must have goals, but our present happiness cannot depend on those goals. We must cultivate happiness right now, whatever our circumstances, and *before attaining our goals*, in order to successfully achieve those goals. This is the peak state of flow. This is what we seek by making a habit of meditation and reconnecting with nature, and it's also cultivated through the process of creating a business plan because self-confidence rises, and that is innately linked to happiness.

The Importance of Self-Confidence

Dr. Lewis Terman, inventor of the Stanford-Binet IQ test, conducted a longitudinal investigation of 1,528 gifted children with IQs at the genius level. The objective was to understand better the relationship between human intelligence and human achievement. The study became famous for its discovery that intelligence was the lesser of several factors that determine achievement. *Discipline and self-confidence were found to be more important than intelligence for achieving things.*

As you do all the work necessary to turn your winning idea into a real company that fixes problems and improves the world, building and supporting your self-confidence is essential. As I say, this is one goal of building a business plan, but I want to emphasize how easy it can be to let negative information and potential problems derail the process and undermine a positive attitude.

Contrary to what many in the media say, there is never a wrong time to start a business, but there is never a right time, either. There will never be a perfect set of circumstances. The economy peaks and troughs like a roller coaster. Employment figures can fluctuate wildly. Loans can be easy to get one day and hard to get the next. However, half the companies that make up the Dow Jones Industrial Average were started in the midst of a recession. Don't let pundits stop you from starting your business, but use the business-plan process to investigate existing circumstances and strategize how to meet them.

In other words, as you develop your business plan, expect that you will discover unforeseen problems you would otherwise have missed. That's why the business-plan process is so important: It's about gathering information, identifying obstacles, and figuring out how to overcome them before you start. This can take time, and some challenges will be more difficult to overcome than others. Some circumstances may inspire you to adjust your original business plan. That's okay... it's part of the process.

However, don't let these issues or the steady diet of negative information from the media cause a cascade of equally negative thoughts that undermine your resolve. The media thrive on paralyzing us with fear so they can zap us with a dose of commercials, and pundits on TV and the radio can seem convinced that the world is about to end and everyone is out to kill everyone else. That's not the reality I see when I travel, but it can be hard to remain focused on our winning idea when all we hear from the media is doom and gloom. So my suggestion is, if you feel your enthusiasm and self-confidence eroding, stop listening to the media.

Turn the dial, flick the switch, cancel the paper. Your RAS will benefit as you filter out the doomsday peddlers. Go cold turkey on the news if you have to, and listen only to positive, beneficial small-business advice on blogs, podcasts, and so on, ones that provide useful tips and support a positive frame of mind.

We can't stop negative thoughts from arising, or control them when they do, but we have 100 percent control over our reactions to our thoughts. If we hear or see something that causes fear or hurts our self-confidence, we should deliberately choose a more positive reaction.

A Business Plan Focuses on Customers and the Market

What is a business plan? What does it do, and what is the goal? Peter Cohan, a successful investor and author, once stated:

> I started investing in startups in 1996 and have seen plenty of business plans.... I have invested in six start-ups and three of those were sold for a total of $2 billion. The other three went out of business. And even in that tiny sample, there is typically one connection between these successful business plans. Simply put, the successful business plans contained deep insights into the prospective customers. And the ones that failed did not.

That is the best and most concise definition for a business plan that I have ever read. A business plan describes prospective customers and the market potential, and it is written first and foremost as a blueprint for the business owner's own benefit. So many entrepreneurs fall into the trap of thinking that a business plan is an MBA-type thesis designed to impress investors. Entrepreneurs treat the business plan as a way to explain their winning idea. It is the opposite. Instead, after a process of investigation, the plan summarizes, not how great the winning idea is, but who needs it, what problem it solves (that can't be solved without it), how you will get the attention of customers (and convince them to buy), how your product or service fits in the current marketplace, and how the company will be structured to survive financially until your winning idea is the runaway success that you hope.

To get all this information, you need to talk to people. Writing a business plan requires interviewing or surveying

potential customers, particularly those who have used similar products or services recently within the market you will be
joining. You want to learn what they like and don't like, what
they value, and what improvements they'd like to see. Customers have given me some of the best ideas for product improvements and marketing campaigns. It also means investigating
the competition and evaluating what others do well and do
badly, along with figuring out how to distinguish yourself from
what already exists.

Social networks and various web-based analytical tools can
provide basic data for customer profiling, but by themselves,
they rarely provide the deeper insights you need. Your prospective customer is not a set of digital fingerprints. Your customer is a real person with real feelings and opinions that often
cannot be expressed appropriately online. When you research
prospective customers, your goal is not just to understand the
statistical profile of a group but to appreciate the subtle nu-
ances of individual buyers and their thought processes.

What I find odd and disconcerting is that, given all the advice available about this topic, hardly anyone recommends getting away from your desk and actually speaking to people. Many
times, I have listened to a business-plan presentation only to
learn that the entrepreneur has not bothered to discuss anything
with potential customers, distributors, or manufacturers. Many
entrepreneurs think that they can understand their customers
without actually meeting any in person, but those same entrepreneurs are often unable to answer even the simplest questions
with confidence. It shouldn't be a revolutionary idea, but it almost is: As you research prospective customers, meet and greet
real, living-and-breathing human beings.

What people say may surprise you, and what you learn can
provide crucial insight, shortcuts, strategies, and inspiration
that allow you to adapt to and take advantage of the constantly

changing conditions in the marketplace. Ultimately, this reflects one of the "secrets" to success: Successful entrepreneurs adapt to the state of the market and the needs of customers. Yet the ability to adapt and make effective decisions depends on the depth of your knowledge and understanding, which is what you improve through the business-plan process.

For instance, one time I was able to significantly raise the price of a product when I discovered that a larger company had recently increased its price of a product tenfold. I was interviewing a prospective customer who was hopping mad about the larger company's decision and who vented his feelings throughout our conversation. My product was in the same regulatory field, but specifically targeting a different need. I decided to re-price my product significantly prior to launch with the knowledge that I would not draw the same negative attention, since my product would still be priced below the larger company's product. Plus, no one would know I had changed the price.

Another time a prospective customer was assessing the product I intended to launch when she commented that she had seen something similar from a local manufacturer. She showed me a sample hidden away in a drawer. With a little detective work, I found a competitor had illegally entered the market despite the patent protection around my invention. Before that company could create too much market damage, I was able to use my strong patent position to get an injunction on their marketing. Eventually they withdrew from the market altogether. Without the business-plan process, I might not have discovered the competitor until much later.

How to Engage Your Stakeholders

Personally, I find the business-plan process the most exciting part of the startup phase because it requires face-to-face discussions about how to turn an idea into a company. To engage with potential customers, I usually go where I know they will be gathered in large numbers. Typically, that will be at a major exhibition running at a convention center, which is also where lots of my potential competition will be showcasing their products and services. I also go to shopping malls and markets where I can conduct surveys with prospective customers. Sometimes I have rented a small exhibit space at a relevant trade show and conducted a market research survey with attendees. People love to talk about themselves and answer survey questions, especially if I offer free coffee, bagels, or some other gift in return. What I learn in these events often takes my business idea in different directions than I would otherwise have envisaged. This sounds "old school," but it is an essential. There simply is no substitute for a free-flowing conversation between an entrepreneur and a prospective customer.

How do you conduct effective face-to-face research? Do you conduct formal surveys or simply chat to people? How many contacts is enough? There are no rules. I think the right approach really depends on your idea and its related market. I have done all of these things. I find that a generic-style survey with multiple-choice answers results in generic responses. Alternatively, I find that having a casual, friendly chat with a prospective customer using the art of conversation eventually reveals exceptionally deep information about their true feelings. These might not be the feelings I imagined they would have, and I might or might not have thought to include them as an option on a multiple-choice questionnaire, but they are genuine emotionally driven opinions.

People enjoy surveys and quizzes, and the anonymity of the internet can get you more realistic responses through a website or social media group chat than a bland paper survey. That helps, but I feel that to really understand a customer's perspective requires actual human interaction. In all cases, I believe authenticity wins the day. Typically, I'm up-front with people and explain that I'm planning a company to fix a certain problem, and that I don't yet know the answers to all the questions. This gains support and fosters camaraderie. People open up more; as humans, most of us have a natural inclination to want to help the underdog succeed.

I can't say how much information is enough, but I know when my intuition is kicking in and pulling me in a certain direction. When that happens, I have enough data to form a strategy. This is why deepening your intuition is so valuable.

Even if you have started a business already but have avoided going through this process, I recommend you go through it now. It is never too late, and you will never regret making the effort. These conversations teach you so much about how others see you and your business, which is information that gives you the opportunity to mirror, adapt, and improve.

Psychologists say there are three perspectives on ourselves: There is the way we see ourselves, there is the way we think others see us, and then there is the way others actually see us. Only by getting away from our desk and talking face-to-face with our stakeholders can we grasp all three views.

Creating a Business Plan

As I say, the process of researching a business plan is more important than the shape or size of the final document. How you organize and write your plan is less critical than the information you gather through the process.

Many entrepreneurs get bogged down by the idea of the written document. That is not the goal of this whole process. No investor cares if your final document is ten pages or a hundred pages. An investor wants insight. That's the goal. What makes your winning idea different? What need does it serve? What is the market size? How is the investment going to be used? What are the barriers for competitor entry? Why is it exciting?

A potential manufacturing vendor needs to know about your forecasts for growth. A commercial partner wants to know what benefits your product provides to customers and what they in turn think about your prototype. When vendors ask you for the information they need, you typically pull that data from your plan and give them just what they ask for and no more. The information is important, not the document's style, format, size, or even structure. No one cares about the document.

Here's the hard truth: No one but you will ever read the entire business plan. And you will probably only ever read it all through once, on the day it is finished. That's my experience. Investors will read the executive summary. Vendors might read the sections that apply to their role. Later, after you start your company, you'll find that much of your plan will become irrelevant as things surprise you and you adapt to survive. Eventually, the business-plan document you spent so many months writing and stressing over will simply collect dust until one day it gets tossed in the trash to be replaced with an update.

Personally, as an investor, I read the executive summary, and I pretty much make up my mind by the end of that. If I am intrigued, I'll look for what marketing and customer research has been done. If none, it goes in the trash can. That sounds harsh, but it is the real world. Investors receive hundreds if not thousands of business plans every year, and the majority that I receive read like they came straight out of an MBA course. Guaranteed trash-can toss. These days I charge people to submit their plan, and I have to say, that does separate the wheat from the chaff.

Knowing this to be true, many would-be entrepreneurs spend weeks trying to produce a killer executive summary — *but without actually performing the business-plan process.* I repeat, the business plan is *not* a document. It is a summary of the insight you gain through your interactions with customers and vendors. You cannot imagine that information or replace that process, and those executive summaries that try betray themselves within the first few paragraphs.

A successful executive summary only results when an entrepreneur has gone through the full process of researching the business plan. The resulting information is of course collected and organized into a document, but it's the knowledge gained in the process that arms the business owner with the ability to write, present, and pitch that killer executive summary.

My advice is: Don't try to produce a perfect document, since you are the only one who will ever read it. Don't be anxious about following some standard format you find online, and never pay for an online business plan. Research each area I outline below by actually leaving your office and talking to real people in some way, and do so until you feel confident you understand the issues involved and have adequately answered the major questions in your head. Then summarize and explain your findings as succinctly as you can for yourself in the document. That formal action of writing it all down cements the concepts and knowledge in your brain. It is not a step that can be skipped. In general, worthwhile business plans tend to be lengthy documents because you uncover so much useful information. Some so-called experts suggest succinct documents. It doesn't matter. What will sell the plan is the executive summary, and the quality of that cannot be forged with clever writing or MBA-speak.

As for how to begin, one of the best pieces of writing advice I have ever received was that — rather than start at the beginning, write through a middle, and go to the end — it's easier to start writing about whatever you find fun or interesting, and then expand outward from there. Start with a story or an anecdote to get the creative juices flowing and then expand around that core story, filling in the blanks in whatever order that comes to you.

That is how I write business plans (and how I began writing this book): I jump into the middle and start with whatever interests me the most. Since marketing interests me, I usually start there. That leads to thoughts about packaging and manufacturing, and off I go on another voyage of discovery. You can do the same. Start wherever you feel most comfortable, or with whatever inspires you the most, and keep going until you've covered every topic.

Researching Industries, Companies, and Markets

Below, I describe the nine sections or topics that typically appear in most business plans. In addition, plenty of example business plans can be found online to help you get started. However, rather than follow some generic template (even the one in this book), I recommend first researching your industry and market and then organizing the business plan so that it reflects what industry stakeholders care about the most.

How do you do that? Read the annual reports of public companies. Most public companies must disclose corporate information to their shareholders, and they usually do so in a state-of-the-company report. These usually include an opening letter from the CEO, financial data, results of operations, market segment information, new product plans, subsidiary activities, and research-and-development activities on future programs. Reporting companies must send annual reports to their shareholders when they hold annual meetings to elect directors. Under the proxy rules, reporting companies are required to post their proxy materials, including their annual reports, on their company websites.

On company websites, these reports are usually under the shareholder, investor, or financial tabs. Annual reports are really very detailed business plans, and they can be an excellent guide as to the type of content that people care about. It doesn't matter that the company is a multimillion-dollar enterprise. The only difference between you and them is the size of the numbers. Additionally, the data on markets can be relevant to your business, and you get it all for free.

Plus, you may come across additional threats and opportunities. For instance, three years into my first company, I was seeking new acquisitions in the form of abandoned product lines. The only way to find them was by combing through public company annual reports to find ones that stated unequivocally that they had abandoned products for strategic reasons. Although it was a somewhat mind-numbing activity, I read through dozens of reports, and eventually I came across one that warned its shareholders of serious cash-flow issues. Deep into the annual report, it mentioned cost-cutting exercises, such as dismantling its sales team and no longer marketing three of its lower-revenue products. So I seized the opportunity and approached them with an offer to purchase the product rights. I had to raise an additional $28 million, which happened quickly. Ultimately, the deal provided the struggling company with enough cash to survive, and I went on to triple the value of the purchased products.

Another good source of information for overall market statistics, competition, product sales, demographics, and coming innovations are the market research reports that are produced for just about every industry. They can cost hundreds and even thousands of dollars, mainly because lazy middle managers buy them in bulk and plagiarize the contents to impress their sales and marketing bosses with their market-analysis presentations. I know because that is what I used to do.

Fortunately, most senior management don't know that they exist. It is possible, however, with a little online search creativity, to find whole market sections available for free as well as some of those impressive management presentations that summarize the markets, demographics, and current and anticipated competition.

Section by Section:
The Nine Parts of a Business Plan

Most business plans contain nine or so sections that reflect all the major topics or issues that inform the entrepreneur's business strategy. Use this list as a way to organize your investigative research, and then merge topics, retitle sections, and reorder them in whatever way is appropriate for your business. Keep in mind that this is not about completing a section for the sake of it. The goal of the process is to understand the real-world circumstances that impact your winning idea and your company. How you write the plan is up to you, but use the lists of questions below as a guide for what to address. Successful entrepreneurs should be able to answer all of these questions fully if asked by a potential investor in a fund-raising meeting, while supporting those answers with actual stakeholder feedback.

When you feel you're finished, the litmus test for determining the effectiveness of your business plan is to share it with others, such as stakeholders you've interviewed or other knowledgeable people in the industry. Ask for opinions on your proposed marketing plans. Ask potential customers if you have accurately identified their needs and matched them to the real benefits of your product. Then revise the plan as necessary to clarify, improve, and finalize it.

Here are the nine sections:

1. **Executive summary:** This is a short synopsis of the entire plan that answers the question "Why should I care?"
2. **Business description:** This presents the winning idea, the need it fills, and the market potential for the business.
3. **Marketing:** This describes potential customers, competition, pricing strategies, packaging, sales, and marketing.
4. **Manufacturing and distribution:** This describes the infrastructure for actually producing and distributing what you will sell, including backup vendors and budgets against growth forecasts for three years.
5. **Organization:** This briefly describes the company organization, including employees, management, vendors, consultants, and advisors, along with your own background.
6. **Critical risks:** This describes any significant challenges or obstacles and how they will be met, typically using a SWOT analysis (see pages 64–65).
7. **Financial:** This estimates expenses, revenues, and profits, with particular attention to cash-flow challenges.
8. **Milestone schedule:** This describes the planned schedule and any significant deadlines for a three-year growth period.
9. **Appendix:** This provides any supporting documents as necessary.

1. Executive Summary

When your goal is to attract business partners — such as investors — you need to create two succinct descriptions of your business. One is a single-page executive summary of your business plan, which gets sent to potential investors; the other is the "elevator pitch," a shorter, verbal version of the written summary that you use when someone says, "I heard you have a great idea for a business. What is it?"

First, let's discuss the executive summary. Budding entrepreneurs sometimes make the same mistake of many job seekers when they send me unsolicited résumés that are pages long. I'm busy, and without a compelling reason to consider someone, I'm not going to spend the time to review their entire work history. Further, the more detailed information I read, the more opportunity I have to make unchallenged judgments and find reasons to disqualify the person as a candidate. A good résumé highlights the most relevant qualifications, providing just enough information to intrigue me and make me want to call the candidate to learn more.

That is what a good executive summary does. In one page, it overviews the key data you discovered by going through the lengthy business-plan process that makes you excited and confident about your winning idea. If you do the process well, the one-page summary will all but write itself. However, there are lots of examples online; just do an internet search for "brilliant executive summaries." There is no perfect style. What will make or break yours is how well you know your market. In addition, everything you include in the summary should be explained or supported in more detail elsewhere in the plan. Here are the main topics to address and questions to answer:

- What is the overall size of the market in dollars? (Which you can research using market reports.)
- What is your niche? What customer need will you satisfy?
- What is the market potential? (For investors, use only big numbers.)
- Who are the customers, and why will they be delighted?
- How is your company different from other similar companies?

- How much capital will be required, and how will it be used?
- What phases of growth and milestones do you anticipate?
- What is the anticipated return on the investment?
- Why is the venture a good risk?

The Elevator Pitch

While your business plan's executive summary overviews all the key points of the plan, you also want to distill this even further into a one-minute verbal pitch with a catchy tagline intended to "hook" the person you're talking to. The concept for an elevator pitch is to imagine stepping into an elevator at the same time as a woman with a million dollars in her pocket, but she doesn't know where to invest it. To sell her your idea, all you get is the time it takes for the elevator to reach her destination. In vivid, passionate terms, you want to encapsulate your winning idea, why it's sure to succeed, and what the investor will get out of it (or the return on her investment).

This is no easy thing to do. It requires much practice to distill the essence of your winning idea and business concept in this way. In reality, you do not even get a minute. It's more like thirty seconds.

For example, on my website you'll find the catchy tagline "Where transformation and financial independence meet." If anyone asks me about my concept for courses and books, that is it in a nutshell. In that mythical elevator, I'd say: "It's about where transformation and financial independence meet; if you'd like more details, I'd be happy to send you the course summaries. What is your best email address to use?"

Done. Next floor, please.

2. Business Description

In this section, describe the winning idea fully. Describe the type of business and the specific product or service. Describe the critical need it fulfills and why customers will be delighted to buy it. Explain what makes it unique or different from the competition. Summarize the market potential based on referenced research and customer feedback, and estimate how quickly investors will get a return on their investment. See also "What Makes a Winning Product or Service," pages 178–81.

- What type of opportunity is it?
- Why does it promise to succeed?
- What is the growth potential?
- In what ways is it unique?
- How does it compare to others?

3. Marketing

This section describes your potential customers and how you will reach them and convince them to buy, and it shares the customer feedback you've already received. Define your specific market segment or niche in as much detail as possible. For instance, all humans drink, but only some drink sodas, and of those, only some drink diet sodas, and of those, only some drink sugar-free sodas. These are all segments. What is your segment? For help, read annual industry market reports, which describe their market niches.

For more on marketing, see "The Recipe for Great Marketing," pages 185–91; "Outsourcing Direct Sales," pages 204–6; and "Affiliate Marketing," pages 206–7.

- Do you have preorders?
- Who are your competitors? How are their businesses positioned? What do they do well?

- What market share do you anticipate by year one, two, and three based on the responses you received from customer conversations? How quickly will customers adopt your service or product, and what tactics will ensure rapid adoption?
- How will you price your product or service? What do customers say about price? Will you use incentives to encourage buying sooner? How will you ensure quick payments? (For more on this, see "Set a Fair Price," pages 221–22, and "Make Purchasing Easy," pages 227–29.)
- What advertising and promotional strategies will you use to generate leads and sales? Why have you chosen them? How have you tested potential effectiveness? (For more, see chapter 7.)

4. Manufacturing and Distribution

Describe how you will make and distribute the product, along with the costs involved (which likely vary by volume). For any and all manufacturers and vendors you plan to work with, provide their business history and current financial standing. I also recommend identifying backup providers in case your main one goes out of business.

- Who will make the product and at what cost? Describe the manufacturer, along with any backup providers.
- Who will ship the product and at what cost?
- What steps are required to produce your product or service?
- If you plan to manufacture yourself, who will be your suppliers? Costs, vendor stability, and experience?
- What is the availability of labor and materials?

5. Organization

Describe who will manage the business, the company organization, and the roles of all employees, consultants, and advisors. In chapter 6, I describe the hub model that I recommend for startups, but whatever your situation, keep this short. For yourself as the owner and CEO, and for anyone else in your management team (mine have always been part-time consultants), provide summary résumés.

- As the CEO, what experience do you have?
- How will you structure your organization and why?
- What consultants and specialists will you need? How will you use them and what will they cost?
- What legal form of ownership will you choose? (See chapter 2 for incorporation advice.)
- What licenses and permits will you need?
- What facilities are essential, and what do they cost?
- If you have board members and advisors, what value do they bring? How will you meet and at what frequency?

6. Critical Risks

There is no such thing as a risk-free business. In this section, anticipate foreseeable problems and obstacles, as well as potential opportunities. In particular, explain financial issues related to cash flow (chapter 4) and raising sufficient capital (chapter 5). But this can also include potential competitor responses to your market entry, any challenges of organic expansion, inflation and rising supplier costs over time, and the patentability of your product and any barriers to new competition.

Investors will require you to provide what is called a SWOT analysis, which stands for strengths (S), weaknesses

(W), opportunities (O), and threats (T). Investors know you cannot predict everything that might happen, but they need to know you have at least considered potential outcomes and done your due diligence. This is equivalent to kicking the tires on the car you've just built. A SWOT analysis is usually presented as a simple table or list:

Strengths could be: *First-in class invention, lengthy patent protection, fixing or improving a situation, preorders.*

Weaknesses could be: *Lengthy development process, uncertainty in manufacturing or sourcing of supplies, high price.*

Opportunities could be: *Product expansion markets, economies of scale, global audience.*

Threats could be: *Unknown technology, state or government regulation changes.*

7. Financial

No investor will believe you can get the financials right, but they want to see that you have made a deep analysis and considered cash flow (see chapters 4 and 5). This section is basically a spreadsheet that attempts to capture all expenses and anticipated revenue growth over three years. Provide estimates of fixed expenses (like consultant and vendor management fees) and of variable expenses (volume shipping and manufacturing, increased hiring for growth). Provide revenue and profit forecasts, and describe any cash-flow challenges.

This is always a guessing game. If you are not used to making spreadsheets, there are plenty of courses available. You'll find it a much-used skill in your business, so it is worth the investment to learn.

- What is your total estimated business income for the first year? Monthly for the first year? Quarterly for the second and third years?
- What are the full expenses of the business by week and month for the first twelve months?
- What is the anticipated revenue flow over time?
- What will it cost you to start the business?
- How will you cover personal financial needs?
- What sales volume will you need in order to make a profit the first three years?

8. Milestone Schedule

Some businesses, like research and development, are dependent on reaching milestones before they can be sold. What are the milestones, and when do you anticipate reaching them?

9. Appendix

The appendix is the place for all important documents, such as the incorporation certificate, articles of incorporation, drawings of prototypes, diagrams of the business model, agreements with vendors, stakeholder feedback from interviews and surveys, résumé summaries for the management team and advisory board, and anything else that seems useful.

Every Business Plan Is a Work in Progress

Once you finish your business plan, the most important thing to remember is that business never goes according to plan.

For example, I doubt William Wrigley Jr. ever wrote a business plan, but if he had, it would have focused on Chicago's soap market. In the spring of 1891, at age twenty-nine, Wrigley moved from Philadelphia to Chicago and — with only thirty-two dollars to his name — started a new business selling Wrigley's Scouring Soap. This made sense, as Wrigley's father was a soap manufacturer, but demand was slow. To encourage merchants to stock the Wrigley brand, he offered free baking powder with every purchase. To his surprise, the incentive was more popular than the soap. So he changed his plan and began selling baking powder instead. Because incentives had worked so well before, Wrigley made an offer to every customer of two packets of chewing gum with each can of baking powder. It wasn't long before the gum became more popular than the baking powder, and Wrigley adapted his business again. In 1893, he started selling his own brand of chewing gum and in several flavor choices.

This is a great story. Chewing gum was probably the furthest thing from Wrigley's mind when he started his business, but it was the product that made him a success. Though Wrigley lived in an era when things changed more slowly than they do today, he still adapted three times in three years and mostly followed his intuition. Today, entrepreneurs must adapt much faster, but the lesson remains the same. As soon as they open their doors, most businesses have to adapt to the reality of the market and adjust their plans to survive.

In other words, the business plan is not a one-off. It's a process, a constant work in progress, and I recommend reviewing and updating your plan annually. The *Harvard Business Review* magazine regularly makes the point that to survive long enough to hit a home run, a company must reinvent itself periodically, jumping from the flattening end of one business performance curve to the rising slope of another. Very few companies make the leap successfully when the time comes. That's because they start the reinvention process too late. After a stall sets in, the odds against recovery rise dramatically with the passage of time.

Thus, it's important to continually track the market and competition, to review how well you are serving your customers, and to plant the seeds for new businesses before revenues from existing ones begin to stall. This is how companies enjoy sustained high performance. When your budget permits, it is a good idea to purchase an annual subscription to whichever company writes and sells the annual market research report for your business. They can be invaluable in providing insight into emerging opportunities and threats. In your internet browser, search for the top-ten global market research report providers and go from there.

After completing the process each year, it is also a good idea to use the updated executive summary to hold annual reviews with all your vendors, suppliers, and manufacturers. The attitude you want to create is one of teamwork by seeking continuous improvement from those you rely on for services. Share your success with them and thank them for being part of it.

PART II

SURVIVING

It is not the most intellectual of the species that survives;
it is not the strongest that survives; but the species that
survives is the one that is best able to adapt and adjust
to the changing environment in which it finds itself.

— LEON C. MEGGINSON

When I first started out as my own boss, a seasoned entrepreneur whispered in my ear that "the secret" was to survive long enough to hit a home run. I did not really understand his tongue-in-cheek advice at the time, but I do now. If a startup can somehow make it through the difficult early days, it might live to enjoy the good times. Three of my companies were started in a period of economic recession. Markets and economies fluctuate, and every industry will have upswings and downswings. The "secret" to surviving these ups and downs is money management.

That is the focus of part 2, which explores three topics: cash flow, finding investors, and staffing. Most startups don't survive because they mismanage cash flow, and they spend too much cash too soon on infrastructure and people.

On paper, cash flow is remarkably simple, and academics have written dozens of books on the topic. If you spend less than you take in, you will survive. It is, however, remarkably tricky to manage cash flow in the real world of the startup, and it is well documented that among all companies, large or small, 82 percent fail due to cash-flow issues.

Then, it is common for startups, particularly early in the

company's growth, to bring in investors, who offer needed extra funds in exchange for a share of ownership. For many owners who prefer bootstrapping, this can be a difficult but necessary trade-off to succeed in our current "get big fast" business culture.

Finally, what do most companies do with those investor funds? Typically, they hire people — usually too many people. I recommend saving that precious cash for market growth by adopting a hub structure for startups, which means contracting a "virtual" workforce rather than hiring employees. It does not have to be virtual forever, but this is a great way to start out.

With survival assured, you can then start to think about what it takes to hit that home run, and part 3 is all about what makes winning companies successful.

CHAPTER FOUR

Cash Flow Is King

We've demonstrated a strong track record of being very disciplined with the use of our cash. We don't let it burn a hole in our pocket. We don't allow it to motivate us to do stupid acquisitions. And so I think that we'd like to continue to keep our powder dry because we do feel that there are one or more strategic opportunities in the future.

— STEVE JOBS

As a general rule of thumb, the Small Business Administration states that new businesses have about a 40 percent chance of surviving for three years or more, and most failures occur within the first two years. After that, the rate of business failure slows, but most businesses never make more than $50,000 in annual receipts in any year. These are depressing statistics, but that does not need to be you.

In my own businesses, the first two years of growth have always been a bumpy ride. The early years are a roller coaster of stress and exhilaration, since it takes time to iron out the wrinkles of the market, to negotiate favorable terms with vendors, and to smooth cash flow so that you always have enough money coming in to cover the money going out.

Initially, managing cash flow is the highest priority for

startups. Cash flow touches a lot of bases; it involves every aspect of the way you run your business. You need to anticipate cash-flow issues as you write your business plan and strategize your company organization, and it requires constant vigilance as you manage expenses on a day-to-day basis. Think of your business as a living entity, and cash is the blood that gives it life. It must circulate and flow, and if it stops flowing for any reason, the company can die...and die quickly.

This chapter reviews the various issues related to cash flow, which boil down to two simple imperatives: Ensure you start with enough cash, and then make sure expenses don't outpace income.

Part of the Plan: Strategize Cash Flow from the Beginning

As entrepreneurs, we need to ensure more money flows in than flows out of the business before the initial capital reserve is depleted. That seems obvious, but it is not so easy to achieve. Success starts with the business plan and how the company is conceived and structured from the ground up. It involves every choice we make, from infrastructure, inventory, employees, investors, product development, and marketing to how much we pay ourselves. Typically, entrepreneurs make large up-front investments that use up most available cash, and they bet their ongoing survival on the hope that incoming revenue will match sales forecasts.

This is yet another reason that it's imperative to go through the full business-plan process. We need to run financial projections and get investors on board early if we don't have enough cash for all the necessary initial expenses. We need to research potential customers and test market products before building infrastructure or leasing storefronts. Potential customers have a way of grounding us, especially when it comes to practical matters like pricing and packaging. Too many companies use up all their capital perfecting a product and preparing it for the market only for it to be met with ambivalence at launch.

This is a cash-flow issue, and my rule of thumb is that, well before capital reserves are depleted, the decision has to be made that good enough is good enough to satisfy the potential customer. In other words, even if the prototype can be improved, so long as it meets the customer's needs, get the product in the market and generate revenue. Then use revenue or raise more capital to upgrade over time.

Another factor that has a significant impact on cash flow is company organization. Employees, office space, and infrastructure all generate significant ongoing expenses, and for startups, I recommend eliminating or minimizing these as much as possible. This is why I suggest using the "hub" model and creating a virtual business, which I describe in chapter 6. One of the main advantages of this structure is the preservation of cash during the bumpy first couple of years. Using this model, the entrepreneur can purchase services and supplies only as needed and easily ratchet production up or down as demand dictates. It does not mean that the company has to remain this way forever, but it is a sensible, sustainable approach that allows for gradual, thoughtful expansion. Another advantage of the hub model is that it allows entrepreneurs to be more nimble and to adjust quickly to unexpected market conditions. Capital isn't tied up in fixed expenses, and there is no need to call meetings or reach consensus.

Even taxes can affect cash flow, and these can vary substantially depending on the type of corporation you create (see chapter 2). With a limited liability company, certain expenses (such as a portion of your home taxes, bills used for a home office, plus vehicle and travel expenses) can be deducted to offset income on your annual income-tax return. In the first couple of years, it may be preferable to deduct expenses this way than to draw cash from the business to pay for expenditures.

When you start out, prepare cash-flow predictions at least every month. Eventually, you can do them only quarterly, and once you've become established, shift to annually. At the start, however, unnoticed expenses can sneak up on you if you are not tracking carefully. Start your cash-flow projection by adding cash on hand at the beginning of the period with other cash to be received from various sources: Estimate how much cash is coming in from customer payments, interest earnings, service fees, partial collections, and so on. Then analyze every upcoming cash outlay, such as utilities, travel, inventory, equipment, professional fees for contractors and vendors, office supplies, debt payments, advertising, and so on. Finally, and most importantly, review the *timing* of payments versus expenses to make sure your lifeblood continues to flow (see "Cash Flow Is All about Timing," pages 80–82).

When planning your business, keep these tips in mind:

- Do not hire an employee until absolutely necessary, and even then second-guess your decision. Do as many jobs as you can yourself (see "Part of the Plan: Get Cross-Function Experience," pages 137–41).
- Teach yourself bookkeeping and get a simple accounting software program, or hire a local, cheap, part-time service.
- Keep travel and meeting costs to a minimum. Challenge your decision to call any face-to-face meeting.
- Do not draw living expenses from the company for as long as possible (see "Personal Sacrifice: Forgoing Compensation," pages 84–85).
- Do not lease office space or equipment unless your product or service relies on it (see "Part of the Plan: Avoid Leasing Office Space," pages 153–54).

- Where possible, negotiate longer payment terms with suppliers and vendors (see "Hiring Vendors and Contractors," pages 144–45).

Be Real about Revenue Projections

In any startup, there is always a leap of faith involved, and most entrepreneurs are optimistic by nature. There is always a danger, however, of what I call "buying your own BS," by which I mean that we are often so enthusiastic for our success that we ignore danger signs and problems that threaten to dull our rosy view of the future. It is not so much that our heads are in the sand as that our heads are in the clouds.

I make that mistake myself. Revenues never come close to my buoyant forecasts, but I still can't help being optimistic whenever I set them. I buy my own BS even when I know not to. To temper this and keep my revenue projections more realistic, I revise my initial calculations based on the following formula:

1. Projects often cost twice as much as budgeted.
2. Projects often are twice as complicated as anticipated.
3. Projects often take twice as long as expected.

After adding up whatever that means in terms of time and money, I then halve my sales forecast. Typically, this leads to an overly pessimistic summary of my prospects, but that's okay. One, it's better to be pleasantly surprised than bankrupt. And two, it usually leads me to realize that whatever capital I have is not going to be enough, and so I raise that capital first, before I need it.

Cash flow is a simple-enough concept to grasp, and endless books address it, but our own unrealistic expectations and desires still lead to bad habits of cash-flow management. Companies of all sizes go bankrupt at an alarming rate, and the Hall of Fame for cash-flow fiascos includes some eminent names. One of my favorite cautionary stories concerns an entrepreneur named Adam Osborne. He built a successful computer-book publishing company, which he sold to McGraw-Hill. Then, using $100,000 of his profits and a loan from a venture capitalist of $40,000, Osborne started a pioneering personal computer company called Osborne Computer Corporation.

Founded in 1981, the company sold the first inexpensive portable computer. The Osborne 1 weighed twenty-four pounds and was the size of a sewing machine. In fact, it looked a bit like one. It had a carrying handle and would fit under an airplane seat. It did not have a battery, so it could not be used in-flight, but executives finally had a way to take their office files with them.

Dealers were enthusiastic, and the first units shipped in June 1981. By August 1982, the company had sold $10 million worth of computers. In February 1983, its sales on the books reached $100 million. By all measures, the company had the fastest growth in computer sales history.

In 1983, however, Osborne preannounced to customers several next-generation computer models, which had not yet been built, and they highlighted the fact that they would outperform the existing model. Sales of the Osborne 1 fell as sharply as they had risen as customers canceled their orders in anticipation of those more-advanced systems.

Stuck with a mountain of suddenly unwanted and obsolete inventory, Osborne reacted by drastically cutting prices on the Osborne 1. Customers, however, did not want to buy an inferior model no matter how discounted.

In June 1983, *InfoWorld* published a story that said the company was suffering from a cash crunch, and that delays with the new machine had hurt Osborne 1 sales. By then, lay-offs began. In July, the *Wall Street Journal* published another story saying that financial woes had forced the company to give up on plans to go public.

> Sales of its Osborne 1, a best seller in 1982, fell off sharply in the spring, when the offering was to have been made, forcing the company into a cash squeeze. Osborne Computer's main problem has been the timing of its introduction of a new portable computer this spring. Dealers cut off orders for the Osborne 1 to wait for the new machine, but it was behind schedule.
>
> "We had an April with no income," says Adam Osborne, the chairman. The company was also coming out of fiscal 1982 with flat results or a loss, and competition from newcomers in the portable-computer business was intensifying. Osborne takes the blame for the introduction snafu.

This type of market event — a preannouncement of a new product causing a drop in demand for older ones — is now known as "the Osborne Effect," but the real reason for Osborne Computer's bankruptcy in September 1983 was poor cash-flow management. That was the reason that Thom Hogan, an executive at Osborne Computer, later cited:

> Cash flow, basically. And decisions relating to it. The company was undercapitalized from the beginning, so the very rapid growth essentially had us ordering more supplies every month faster than we were taking in money on the income side. The company would have sold even more than we did with more capital. Basically

it was "buy as much new parts and add as much staff as we can afford" every day. I can't remember a month where the cash flow numbers looked great, despite the profitability numbers looking decent.

The problem was exacerbated when the board replaced Osborne with an executive from the Coca-Cola company. Osborne had agreed to a deal to sell all the surplus inventory, but the incoming president canceled the deal, stating, "Real companies don't sell inventory at cost." It is possible that the short-term flow of cash from the deal might have saved the company.

It is a bit of a sad story, and I thought long and hard about including it in this book. If I just added rags-to-riches stories, however, the book would be less useful. Part of the problem with cash flow is that most people think they are good at it, whereas in reality most people surround themselves with personal debt in the form of mortgages and credit cards. They quite accept ongoing debt, but in business, that approach is less likely to work.

In Osborne's case, they had produced a successful, profitable product, but they still went bankrupt because they didn't have enough cash to support themselves through a crisis. In any company, large or small, there are always unexpected events that can impact cash. Cash buys time to recover. This may be the final lesson: Once cash flow becomes dire, it's already too late to find investors.

Cash Flow Is All about Timing

Financial accounting is not focused on cash flow. It is focused on net income or profit. Over the long term, profit and cash flow will be approximately the same, but as Osborne discovered, the crucial difference is timing.

The timing of when money goes out and revenues come in is critical, but this is hard to predict at the outset, especially for a startup. This is the real issue of cash-flow management. Typically, money flows out a lot faster than it comes in during the early stages of the business. Customers prefer to buy now and pay later, whereas suppliers have little tolerance for late payments, especially when they know you are new and without a successful payment record. Businesses need enough capital to bridge the time gap, and they need to minimize that gap as much as possible — such as by minimizing infrastructure costs (in terms of inventory, buildings, and staff) and by offering incentives to customers for early payment, such as offering free gifts like "buy now and get this one-time offer."

For example, when you make a sale to a customer, that sale is immediately recognized on your income statement: *Joe Blog bought one widget for $1,000.* That's called accrual accounting, and your system might automatically order a replacement product to be ready for the next sale. Say the cost of manufacturing and shipping is $200. You have now spent $400 because your supplier insists on immediate payment. However, you don't always get the money from that sale immediately — such as if the customer purchased using a subscription-type payment or took advantage of your marketing offer to "buy now, pay later" or "pay in three easy installments." Until you actually receive the full payment, which could be some time off, you are doubly invested, having produced two products for $400 cash out of pocket, but with only one sale yet to be paid for and no money in hand.

Multiply this over and over, and the gap between profit and cash flow in the early stages could be very large. If you have rapid growth in credit sales, for example, profit could far exceed actual cash received. This sort of situation makes smaller companies very vulnerable to running out of cash, especially when one has to pay for manufacturing and supplies in anticipation of demand. Cash flow is nigh on impossible to predict accurately.

That is why you must be more like Ebenezer Scrooge and monitor every unnecessary expense. If any expenditure is not *essential* for your company's survival, it has no place in your business.

Depending on your business, one way you can address this is to offer customers incentives to pay early. That does not mean visiting their homes with a baseball bat in hand. Instead, give a small discount to receive early payment on invoices. Some customers want sixty or ninety days or more to pay, but as a small company, you cannot afford that delay. Then, make it easy for customers to pay straightaway by accepting all manner of payments, and when possible, take deposits when orders are placed. Various online software programs exist to make online payments or bank-to-bank transfers a breeze. Invoices can be generated automatically.

As for supplier or manufacturing invoices that you need to pay, set up last-day payment. Don't be late, but why pay in fifteen days when they don't start assessing interest until day thirty?

Finally, if customers are overdue in their payment once, chances are that they will always be late or deficient. The time you spend chasing these customers can be detrimental to the business. It is better to drop deficient clients and spend the time recruiting new ones.

Beware of Hidden Startup Costs

Here's yet another reason to go through the business-plan process: It will help you identify any unexpected, latent, or "hidden" costs that new entrepreneurs sometimes don't know about. For instance, investors in small businesses usually require keyman insurance coverage, so that if the founder of the business is incapacitated, the investors have some recompense for potential lost profit.

In addition, Western vendors, such as manufacturers and distributors, normally require a minimum level of liability insurance before they will enter into a contract. This is not always the case in Asia. Because manufacturers often deal with many large companies, their minimum level can be several millions, the insurance for which can run into tens of thousands a year. Every industry has companies that specialize in product liability insurance, and it pays to shop around. In my current business, the minimum level is $5 million, and I was quoted prices from $15,000 to $300,000 a year. The better-quality policy turned out to be the cheapest. Though you can try to negotiate down the minimum coverage, larger vendors are not very flexible on terms. If a distributor refuses to stock your product because you don't have sufficient insurance coverage, there is not much you can do but agree to get it.

A company often also needs licenses or permits to operate in different states. The costs are not always proportional to the size of the business, and the process of application can be complicated, time-consuming, and require expert legal help. Permits are often required even before revenues can be received.

Government agencies require the use of surety bonds in a number of different industries, especially those that offer services to consumers. Surety bond regulations are put in place to keep unqualified professionals from accessing certain markets, thus deterring unethical business practices. Unfortunately, new business owners might not realize they even need a surety bond until they're in the middle of the licensing process, and they can be costly.

Personal Sacrifice:
Forgoing Compensation

Entrepreneurs have to be prepared to make sacrifices at the beginning, and a tricky question to consider is how much to pay yourself. For many, this topic is a bit of a reality check. Few startups can support paying the owner any salary at all, much less one that's comparable to a corporate job. For example, with my first company, I did not take a salary or expenses for two years, but I lived on my savings and the profit from the sale of our house. In my third company, I have never taken a salary or expense, and again I was forced to sell our house when a deal fell through and cash flow was threatened. That is the type of sacrifice that startups require in order to survive. If you are not prepared to do that, don't even think of starting a company.

This is one of my pet-hates as an investor. Sometimes I receive a business plan in which the business owner wants a high salary that he or she expects to be covered by the investment. When I review the financial spreadsheet and see that the salary is a significant percentage of the investment, I am immediately put off. Investors call these proposals "lifestyle deals."

No investor wants a starving entrepreneur to run the business. By the same token, any investor expects a business owner to "put some skin in the game." When the business owner has no money of his or her own to invest, that commitment comes in the form of a reasonable compensation package. What is reasonable? Whatever the entrepreneur can sacrifice without jeopardizing their family or personal situation. Ideally, the business owner would forgo any salary at all at the outset and only take compensation from profits. Remember: Revenue is not profit, and actual profit may not be apparent for several months.

As another example, a friend of mine started a media

company. Because his lifestyle includes a large mortgage for the family home and tuition costs for his college-age kids, he withdraws $200,000 a year from the company profits. With annual revenue at around $1 million and business expenses close to $750,000, there is very little profit left for marketing. As a result, the business has remained pretty much the same size for the last decade. The owner has often asked me for help with business strategy, but he refuses to consider changing his lifestyle in the short-term to release money for business growth. If he cut his personal compensation in half, I know he could double his subscriber base and then exit the business through a strategic sale for significant gain. He is, however, in a lifestyle trap. With so little profit showing on the books and flat subscriber growth over many years, the business is simply not financially attractive to a purchaser.

In reality, people often need to withdraw some amount of money to live on, but minimize this as much as possible. Once the bumpy years are over, you will enjoy the fruits of frugality and can make up for that sacrifice. A startup is not a substitute for employment. The longer you can go without drawing much cash out of the business for compensation, the better it will be for the cash flow and your chances of survival.

Manage Expenses by Fostering Frugality

Managing daily expenses starts with fostering an attitude of frugality. To me, this is epitomized by something that Glenn Fleishman, a catalog manager for Amazon in 1996, described about the early days of the company:

> [Bezos] invited me to join Amazon, which I did. But what I remember most was, after lunch, walking into his office in the Columbia Building and seeing a rack

of blue-colored shirts, his trademark at the time, and the door-as-desk. I laughed. I looked at the threadbare carpet and spartan furnishings and said, "Investors must love this." He gave me his patented laugh.

When I joined the company, I saw the door-desks being built all the time.... Jeff told the *Seattle Times*: "These desks serve as a symbol of frugality and a way of thinking. It's very important at Amazon.com to make sure that we're spending money on things that matter to customers.... There is a culture of self-reliance. [With the low-tech desks]...we can save a lot of money."

When running a business, we have to treat every bit of cash as imperative for survival. Challenge every expenditure with the question, "Is this purchase absolutely essential to the survival of my company?"

Wastefulness Is a Corporate Disease

To manage expenses this way can involve recovery from and healing the corporate disease of wastefulness.

Before becoming an entrepreneur, I observed wastefulness in every department in every company I worked for. This arises, I think, mostly because employees are dissociated from the source of the company funds. Employees can lose a sense of personal accountability when money is not coming out of their own pockets. Boy, does that attitude change when you start a company of your own.

Whether the source is investors or profit from customers, most employees never get even close to the people who provide the funds. Once the money hits the company accounts, it usually gets treated as the company's money, and although department and project leaders may be held accountable for budgets, there is far less accountability for the individual employee.

Another idea that can pollute an employee's attitude and foster wastefulness is the feeling that "the company owes me" or "I'm not being paid enough commensurate with my experience." That can lead to deliberate abuse of company funds, especially for business-related expenses. It is almost as if some employees seek payback for a perceived injustice.

The tax system facilitates wastefulness as well. When expenses can be deducted against income, that reduces the tax bill, and this is often the case for the single-person business. Everyone is usually happy about that, but it can lead entrepreneurs to rationalize overspending. What they fail to remember is that the cash is gone right now and any tax savings are in the distant future. Initially, it's much more important to avoid cash-flow problems by not spending if you don't have to.

Wasteful, careless attitudes to budgets and expenses can infect any new business. Entrepreneurs sometimes have little training in bookkeeping, or they can be bad at keeping receipts and accurate records. Thus, they easily lose track of expenses themselves, and that makes managing others and fostering frugal attitudes that much more challenging. If owners simply trust their employees to not be wasteful — and that includes wasting time on personal business and unnecessary meetings — they may be in for a rude surprise. Even when employees are reliable and well-meaning, and not trying to cheat or abuse a startup company, they may not appreciate how seemingly small expenses and acts of wastefulness can add up to a serious drain on cash. This is another area in which the hub model can assist in the early stage of a startup, as contractor and vendor fees and allowable expenses are clearly delineated in the contracts (see chapter 6).

If you think you are immune to this, make a point to go to work tomorrow and give yourself a reality check. Look with fresh eyes, as if you are an outsider. As you walk to your desk, take note of the number of people using company time to complete noncompany business. How many surf the internet before starting real work or make personal calls on a company phone? How often does "getting a cup of coffee" turn into a half-hour discussion of last night's TV shows?

If you hire employees, will they automatically change these habits just because they are working for a new small business? As the owner of your company, you might, since all the costs are now coming out of your pocket. Just make sure that you do, and that you embody and model frugality for everyone who works for you.

Reduce the Company Feel-Good

Another area where we can learn bad habits is with the amount of money invested in programs to increase employee satisfaction in the regular workplace. Classic cases are employee-bonding events that are common at larger firms.

At one company, my first management meeting took place at a luxurious resort in Arizona. With the support staff, senior executive team, and fifty midlevel managers, seventy people took over a five-star hotel for a week.

Every afternoon, time was set aside for golf or sightseeing activities. Every night there were team-bonding exercises that included the handing out of luxury gifts and prizes. The meetings occurred every three months, and the total cost ran into the millions every year. They had become a way of life at the company. Yet all I heard from the attendees at every level were complaints about being away from home too long and the events being an exercise in senior management ego boosting.

In particular, technology startups tend to pile on lifestyle benefits that foster quality of life, partly to compensate for the work demands that are required. However, employees can easily get desensitized to wastefulness and take benefits for granted. As the owner of a startup company, don't feel pressured to provide perks that you can't afford in an effort to make people happy. People will always be happiest to keep their jobs because their company is a success. One way to balance frugality with team bonding is to offer some sort of simple profit-sharing plan.

Grow Slowly: Minimize New Hires

For me, the biggest issue with startups is managing growth in a sustainable way. Many entrepreneurs equate hiring with growth and success, but this is wrong and it can be a fatal mindset.

Think of it this way. When someone builds a new house, do they hire a repairperson to live in the house just in case something needs fixing? No, they wait for something to break, then they hire the appropriate repairperson at an hourly rate. If that person buys one or two more houses — would they need a full-time repairperson then? Probably not. Only when someone owns numerous homes or an apartment complex does it make economic sense to hire someone full-time. Entrepreneurs who embrace the hub model (which I discuss in chapter 6) can be too eager to jettison it at the first signs of success. They hire new employees too quickly, before they are really needed, and jeopardize the startup's early growth.

This was the case at a young company where I worked for a short time. The company was still in the innovation stage, developing and testing potential products. No revenue had been generated, but 25 percent of the annual budget from investor funds was digested by the human resources department, which focused on recruiting, motivating, and appraising staff.

When I joined the company, I met with the senior management team, and I asked a simple question: "What is the company's biggest achievement to date?" Quick as a flash, everyone said as one voice, "We have grown to a staff of fifty-six." The human resources director beamed proudly. That was how they measured their success: in terms of people hired. That is all too common. I have seen many a press release over the years making such an announcement as if it were a major achievement, when in fact, it can often be a warning of impending cash-flow issues.

Most entrepreneurs feel good when they hire people. Our egos get a boost, not just because we are in a position to help someone, but also because we think we are serving communities and society as a whole — even though in our technological society there is no longer a link between employment numbers and economic growth. When this happens, entrepreneurs tend to hire too many people and hire them too early, when the scope of the work required cannot justify the cost. It is far better to restrict hiring until the company is on sound financial footing and when hiring employees does not threaten the day-to-day cash flow. Some industries and markets need employees more than others, but I have had businesses in three unrelated industries and never once hired an employee. Be creative with staffing, and use technology to avoid hiring when you can. It is better to grow slowly, and hire only when the need is urgent, than to hire too many too soon and be forced to lay off those same people or go out of business.

CHAPTER FIVE

Gather Capital and Pitch to Investors

Chase the vision, not the money;
the money will end up following you.

— Tony Hsieh

Starting a company and surviving as a business are two very different phases. You can start a company with nothing more than a few hundred dollars to incorporate an idea. To survive as a business, you need sufficient initial capital to see your winning idea through the startup period of expense-related growth before sufficient revenues start flowing in. In fact, with enough initial capital, all the bumpy, early issues of cash flow described in chapter 4 largely disappear.

Sufficient capital isn't just needed for survival, however. It's necessary for growth. In certain industry sectors like technology, sustainable, expense-managed growth is replaced with an attitude of get big quickly. We live in a world in which upgrades and innovations are an everyday experience. Technology companies no longer have the luxury of taking time to grow. For them and others like them, the objective is to get big as fast as possible and before someone else's winning idea makes your business obsolete. Even if revenue is good during the early years, startups generally do not generate enough cash on their own to fuel rapid growth.

That's the focus of this chapter: gathering the necessary capital to survive as a business and to fund your growth. While you can (and probably will) use your own personal savings, and you may also get bank loans, my recommendation is to convince investors to provide the cash your business needs. I am a big proponent of using external capital, in part because investors bring much more than funds. They provide expertise and a network of contacts that can be like adding fuel to a fire. In addition, when owners don't have the daily stress of paying bills and suppliers, they can focus on what they love and do best: building their business.

What investors ask for in return is a share of ownership. Get used to the idea that your percentage of ownership could become heavily diluted in order for your business to succeed. Some small-business organizations encourage bootstrapping as a way to grow a startup and maintain 100 percent owner-ship, and it's tempting to try, as I know from experience. But the reality is that there are too many cash-flow traps, the need to adapt to unexpected obstacles is too great, and growth is too difficult without sufficient capital. As I like to say, it is better to own 10 percent of a successful company than 100 percent of nothing.

To me, the real question entrepreneurs face is not whether to attract investors. It's how much dilution of ownership is a fair trade-off for what amount of capital. I hope this chap-ter helps you understand the sources of capital, how dilution works, how to value your business, and how to successfully pitch to investors.

How Much Capital Do You Need?

In an *Inc.* survey, 41 percent of CEOs stated that they launched their businesses with $10,000 or less. More than a third of those entrepreneurs started with less than $1,000. Each year's list looks very much like the lists of years past when it comes to the number of founders who started companies with little seed capital. That sounds like a lot of bootstrapping.

How much capital do you need for *your* particular business? Entrepreneur Drew Gerber — who started a technology company, a publicity firm, and a financial planning company — estimates that an entrepreneur will need six months' worth of fixed costs on hand at startup. In an article in *Business News Daily*, he said, "Have a plan to cover your expenses in the first month. Identify your customers before you open the door so you can have a way to start covering those expenses." I don't think this is enough of a comfort zone.

In *Secrets to a Successful Startup*, I am not talking about starting small and creeping toward a $50,000-a-year company. The goal is to build a multimillion-dollar success. That means growth. In chapter 4, I mention the following equation for calculating expenses:

1. Projects often cost twice as much as budgeted.
2. Projects often are twice as complicated as anticipated.
3. Projects often take twice as long as expected.

Replace the word *projects* with *startups*, and the word *often* with *always*, and this becomes my equation for being appropriately capitalized before starting out. In other words, my rule of thumb is that, once you calculate reasonable expenses for the first year of business, double that number, and make sure to have that amount of cash on hand. Almost all cash-flow issues can be cured simply by having unused and unassigned capital at the ready. For instance, let's say that you estimate you need $200,000 for the first-year expenses of your business, and you just happen to have $200,000 in savings. Don't celebrate and open your doors. Get an additional $200,000 first, either from a loan or from an investor. Others might warn you to avoid loans in the early stages because of the pressure to make the payments, but there is no greater pressure than running out of money. When that happens, the business is over, and no bank will lend money to you when they find out you just used up $200,000 and have nothing left. It's always best to ask for money up front while you have leverage.

Types of Costs

On its website, the Small Business Administration has very useful (and free) expense and cost-calculation tools for start-ups; use these (see the endnotes). Here are the various types of expenses to consider when starting your business.

1. **One-time vs. ongoing costs:** One-time expenses will be relevant mostly in the startup process, such as the expenses for incorporating a company, deposits and up-front fees for securing vendor contracts, business software to keep track of order processing, and so on.

2. **Essential monthly costs:** Essential costs are expenses that are absolutely necessary for the company's growth and development, such as the monthly management fee you might pay to your vendors. Optional purchases should be made only if the budget allows.

3. **Fixed vs. variable costs:** Fixed expenses, such as rented equipment, are consistent from month to month, whereas variable expenses depend on the direct sale of products or services.

Is it possible to get as much money as you need? The Small Business Administration's definition of a small business is one with less than five hundred employees, which is a business that I don't consider small at all. A small-business loan, however, is usually quite small indeed, and usually well under $200,000. This is often enough money to survive in the short term, but to fuel growth, startups typically need a lot more.

Sources of Capital

No matter how much you need, the good news is that there is always a plentiful supply of money. Entrepreneurs often tell me, as if it is a fact, that it is impossible to raise money in the current economic climate, which is what they often hear in the media. In fiscal year 2016, however, business loans outstanding for less than $1 million totaled nearly $600 billion. That sounds like a lot of lending to me, and the number has been consistent within a couple of percentage points for two decades.

In their surveys, the National Federation of Independent Business reports that about 40 percent of small businesses cite poor sales as their main business problem. In contrast, only 8 percent report that they can't get all the credit they need. So, money is available, even though it may take a lot of effort to get your hands on it.

Here are the pros and cons of the three main options for raising capital: your savings, banks, and investors.

Using Your Savings

If you already have enough savings to fund your startup costs and also to cover your personal living expenses at the same time, then you might consider moving forward without getting any other financing. Thus you avoid any initial dilution of ownership. However, even in this rosy scenario, there are several reasons you might want to seek outside capital.

First, how much savings is enough? On TV recently, an "investment expert" stated that an entrepreneur should have at least two years' worth of "salary" in their savings account before starting a business. To me, that's a reasonable cushion of cash to live on (separate from funding the business) to get through the bumpy early period as revenues try to catch up with expenses.

Yet I disagree with the suggestion that people should *wait* to start their business until they save that (or some other) amount. Winning ideas cannot afford to wait, and saving is notoriously difficult. Why spend precious time saving money when you could raise outside capital and start running your business right now?

I also question just how many people in any society are in the healthy financial situation of being able to rely on savings to start a business. According to Northwestern Mutual's 2018 *Planning & Progress Study*, the average American now has $38,000 in personal debt, and only 23 percent of Americans are debt free. Add to that the issue of growing household debt — including mortgages and student and vehicle loans — which is widespread across the world, and it becomes easy to see that most people don't have any savings and are struggling to pay their existing debt. This makes getting a bank loan to start a business unattractive, if not impossible. That, however, should not deter you from starting a business. To get startup funding, however, you might need to get a bit creative.

Another thing to consider is that using one's own savings typically means going all in, Texas Hold'em style. Even when people intend to use only some of their savings, a startup business always needs more cash, and so people keep placing bets on themselves and keep putting in more. However, if the business fails — and this can happen through no fault of the entrepreneur — those life savings will be lost for good. Then that startup failure will hurt more than it should. Further, most people's savings are not their own, but their family's. Spending this savings requires 100 percent commitment from everyone, or it can tear relationships apart when things get bumpy.

Finally, a self-funded entrepreneur is also the sole source of knowledge, connections, and experience. When they start out, most entrepreneurs don't know what it is they don't know. That can be dangerous. There is much to be said for bringing in experienced investors who can help us avoid mistakes. For me this is as important as the money they provide.

Getting a Bank Loan

Bank loans are a common source of business capital, but the law requires banks to have collateral before they can lend. Strictly speaking, banks are not supposed to invest in businesses. They are regulated by federal laws to prevent them from using depositors' money in a reckless manner. No one wants their savings invested in risky ventures in which their money could be lost, so banks can't and don't provide loans that are not backed by solid collateral. Startup businesses are not usually safe enough for bank regulators, since startups usually don't have enough collateral, and getting a bank loan for one can be difficult.

That said, small-business financing can be accomplished through bank loans based on the business owner's personal collateral, such as home ownership. Some would say that home equity is the greatest source of small-business financing. That said, using your home as collateral is another type of all-in investment, since if the business fails, the bank will take your home.

It's much easier to get a bank loan after a business has been around for a few years. Once a business has shown stability and acquired enough assets to serve as collateral, banks commonly make loans backed by the business inventory.

An established small business can also turn to specialists to borrow against its accounts receivable. The most common accounts-receivable financing is used to support cash flow when working capital is hung up. Interest rates and fees may be relatively high, but this is still often a good source of small-business financing. In most cases, the lender doesn't take the risk of payment — if your customer doesn't pay you, you have to pay the money back anyhow. These lenders will often review your debtors and choose to finance some or all of the invoices outstanding.

No matter the type of bank loan, however, the biggest downside is that loans require regular repayments, and that is hardly helpful to cash-flow security.

Getting a Loan through a Convertible Note

At the startup phase, a popular and commonly used alternative way to get a loan from family, friends, or angel investors (see below) is through what is known as a convertible note. This is a form of short-term, interest-bearing debt — typically, notes are for one to three years at 5 to 8 percent interest, compounded annually — that converts into equity in the business upon maturity. Usually, maturity is timed in conjunction with a future financing round, at which point the note promises the investor a share based on the final value of the note compared to the valuation of the company at the time of conversion, or an additional share in the value of the company (up to 20 percent is common) at that time. The lender can also simply choose to receive the cash back.

For instance, let's say you start a company and a relative agrees to invest $50,000 to help you get started, with the note converting to 20 percent equity in three years while carrying an interest of 5 percent. At the beginning, no one can really say what the value of your business is, but your relative knows that in three years either they will get a $57,881.25 return — $50,000 times 5 percent compound interest for three years (or at least be owed that by you) — or they will get 20 percent equity in a company that can now have an agreed-upon value. Let's say you did really well, and after three years, the business is valued at $2 million. Your relative converts the note to equity and now owns 20 percent of the business, which represents a value of $400,000. Everyone is happy.

Before a business has started, when it still might be just an idea, it is difficult to value the company. By using a convertible note, you avoid this difficult discussion and receive investment funds without giving up any equity yet and without the need for repayments for three years. Rather, the amount of the loan (plus any accrued interest) converts to equity several years later, after the business is established and when a precise valuation can be determined. As I say, this typically occurs when a startup raises its first round of external financing, which is known as series A financing. (As an aside, rounds of financing are given alphabetical terms. The initial founder funding is often called seed funding; the first external investment is called series A financing; the second round of financing, usually to fund growth, is called series B, and so on.)

Convertible notes are relatively simple to set up because they avoid the sticky topic of the current value of an untested startup (which I discuss below). I have used them in the startup phase myself. I find them to be quick, simple ways to bring a cushion of cash into the company without having to worry about equity or value. Legal fees are also inexpensive for this type of loan. Not every investor likes them, and you'll find some speaking against them online, but it is easy to be critical of debt mechanisms when one does not need the money. Many investors like myself do like them because the upside potential if the company bursts from the gate can be significant.

Attracting Angel Investors and Venture Capital

Angel investors are individuals with a high net worth, or groups of such individuals, who invest *their own* money in a startup business in exchange for a share of ownership. Capital amounts are typically from several thousand dollars up to $2 million, and they usually expect an ownership share, or a return on investment (ROI). In general, angel investors expect to get their money back within five to seven years with an annualized internal rate of return (IRR) of 20 to 40 percent.

A venture capitalist (VC) is a person or company that invests *other people's* money in startup firms and small businesses with perceived long-term growth potential. They typically provide much higher amounts of capital — from $2 million to any amount justified by the market potential, the team's track record, and the originality of the disruptive idea — but they want a larger share of ownership, a higher return on investment (from 25 to 75 percent), and more involvement in how the company is run. Most venture capital comes from groups of wealthy investors, investment banks, and other financial institutions that pool such investments or partnerships and hire someone to invest it for them. Many global, established companies also have venture capital divisions that seek out breakthrough ideas to invest in.

This form of raising capital is popular among new companies or ventures with limited operating history, which cannot raise funds through bank loans. The downside for entrepreneurs is that they dilute their share of ownership, and venture capitalists usually get a say in company decisions. Most VCs prefer companies with boards of directors and an executive hierarchy. I find that those VCs I speak to do not grasp the concept of the hub model very well, which unnerves them (see chapter 6).

I am a proponent of selling ownership for cash because that capital doesn't need immediate repayment, so the funds do not impact cash flow. Investors are repaid through company profit distributions when appropriate as well as a percentage of ownership when the company is sold or launched as a public offering, and so their incentive is for the business to succeed long enough to provide an adequate return on their investment. Unlike a bank, investors are at risk of losing their investment if the business fails, so they like to complete due diligence on any company they invest in. They want to see a detailed business plan that provides a thorough objective test for the merits of the winning idea. This is a good thing, since the more people who do due diligence, the sharper the business plan gets.

In addition, investors usually bring experience to a business, and they are willing and eager to share it. They may have industry or technical knowledge of your markets, as well as networks with additional lenders and potential new customers. Some also provide in-house value-added services, such as accounting and tax preparation. Even if they don't have direct experience of your market, investors bring "fresh eyes." That means no preconceived notions, which can lead to creative solutions.

In my businesses I have experienced going it alone using all my savings as well as raising capital from angel investors and venture capitalists. My stress levels are significantly lower when I build a company with other people's money, rather than my own, but perhaps that is a personal thing. I always feel that with my own money, if I hit a cash-flow crisis, the business could fail, whereas investors have the ability to find ways out of the issues even if it means investing additional cash.

Dilution of Ownership: What It Means

In April 1976, Apple was founded by three people: by Steve Jobs, who it is said invested $1,500 in proceeds from the sale of his vehicle; by Steve Wozniak, who invested $250 from the sale of his Hewlett-Packard 65; and by Ronald Gerald Wayne, who was given a 10 percent stake in Apple but sold out for $800 only two weeks later.

Wayne joined Apple cofounders Wozniak and Jobs, who were then twenty-one and twenty-five, to provide "adult supervision" and to oversee mechanical engineering and documentation. Yet soon after sitting down at his typewriter and drawing up an agreement outlining each man's responsibilities, Wayne grew concerned that any debts incurred by the business would fall on him personally. Jobs had taken out a $15,000 loan so he could buy supplies to fulfill Apple's first contract with a Bay Area computer store, which had ordered around a hundred computers. But Jobs and Wozniak were young and broke, and if the computer store failed to pay its bills, and Apple couldn't pay back the loan, Wayne's assets, including his house, might be seized. Wayne sold his percentage share back for $800. Today, that 10 percent share would be worth about $95 billion, but Ron Wayne is openly pragmatic and accepting about it in his many interviews.

About a year later, in 1977, Apple was incorporated at the request of venture capitalist Arthur Rock and ex-Intel manager Mike Markkula. Markkula brought his business expertise along with $250,000 ($80,000 as an equity investment in the company and $170,000 as a loan), and he received one-third of company ownership in exchange for the cash. The investment helped Apple survive and then flourish.

In 1980, Apple went public, and it generated more capital than any IPO since Ford in 1956, and it instantly created three hundred company millionaires. At that point, the exchange of equity for a small amount of cash seemed like a good deal to everyone involved.

By this time, Steve Jobs's ownership had been diluted to 13.5 percent, and Steve Wozniak's to 7.1 percent. While that seems small, it is typical for business ownership. Raising investment capital often requires the owner or owners to significantly dilute their share of ownership. The two founders of Google own 16 percent of the company between them, and even Bill Gates only owns 40 percent of Microsoft. eBay's two founders have 30 percent and 20 percent ownership, respectively.

My Experience of Raising Capital and Dilution

After coming up with my first winning idea, which I describe in chapters 1 and 2, I resigned from my regular job and a few days later called the company's CEO with an offer to purchase the company's smallest asset. I had incorporated my business as TGB International LLC and spent several weeks drawing diagrams on napkins; interviewing potential customers, manufacturers, and marketers; and fleshing out my first business plan.

The asset I wanted to buy generated less than $700,000 a year in sales and was not very profitable. I believed I could manage the asset differently to increase sales and boost profitability. I offered $2.1 million in cash, or three times the annual revenue, for the rights purchase, which was a fair market price for such a deal at that time. The challenge was that I had only $30,000 in savings.

The CEO was not strong at making decisions. He had spent his career in finance, and he understood very little about the rest of the company's functions. He had hired a team of executives with big titles like "senior executive vice president," over fifty other staff, and leased two floors of an expensive office complex. The company was not cash-flow positive, and the share price was at an all-time low.

I knew that the cash I was offering would help save their company, but I also knew that the company's decision-making process was very slow. As I waited for their response, and anticipating a successful outcome, I set about finding an investor.

Banks gave me little encouragement. They struggled with the fact that the business model I proposed (based on the hub model) had never been tried before. They said that I had never been a CEO or owned a company, and they turned me down. I had no rich relatives to beg from, and few assets of my own to sell or leverage. I sold my house, but that provided only enough money for a year's living expenses.

After three months, my former employer finally replied and turned down my offer. By that time, I had traveled thousands of miles presenting my business plan to over twenty potential investors, and each one had also rejected me.

Yet I still felt encouraged. I knew the company's cash-flow issues would only get worse, and the day would come when the executive team would realize that without an acute injection of cash, their jobs would be in jeopardy. Plus, even though each investor I spoke to ultimately said no, most reacted positively to my pitch. From their feedback, I concluded that I needed to demonstrate a working model, or a sort of proof of concept. So I adjusted my business plan. I figured out that I could purchase a different asset from my previous company, which generated only $40,000 a year in revenue, for about $60,000, plus I would need an additional $30,000 working capital to execute the marketing plan.

I convinced two friends to invest in TGB International LLC, and we each contributed $30,000. Immediately, my ownership share changed from 100 percent to 33.33 percent, but I had the investment I needed to start my business.

Although the product provided only a small revenue stream, I was able to build my virtual business model using the entire "hub and spoke" structure I describe in chapter 6. I was the sole "employee," and I lined up contract manufacturers and distributors, and I outsourced accounting, regulatory, and customer services. Within a few months, I'd gotten a handful of new customers and increased profitability. Now investors could better envisage how a larger-scale business using this approach would work. They understood that what I had created was a sort of plug-and-play business model for small-revenue products.

Eventually, as I expected, my old company became desperate for cash. By then, I was able to secure an investment of $2.1 million in exchange for 70 percent ownership. If, however, I could pay back the investment within six years, the ownership would switch to 70/30 in my favor. Because I had two partners in the business already, my ownership share would be only one-third: either 10 percent (one-third of 30 percent) or 23.33 percent (one-third of 70 percent), depending on the outcome after six years.

Turning 100 percent ownership into 33.33 percent and then 23.33 percent takes courage, but the external funding and working capital gave me the fuel to build a successful company. Within three years the company was producing $10 million a year in top-line revenue with profits over 75 percent. We paid back the investment within six years, and everyone was happy.

With the company a proven success, we used its new valuation to justify a senior debt loan of $28 million in order to acquire three more assets (as I mention in chapter 3) and expand the business even faster — and this time with no further dilution of ownership. ("Senior debt" means senior to other investors, in that when cash is available, the "senior" loan gets paid off first before other investors get their hands on the remaining cash.)

With my next company, I had the cash to go it alone for a few years. Then having created a reasonable valuation, I sold two-thirds ownership in exchange for cash and resources. This time reducing 100 percent ownership to 33 percent was an easy decision because the value had already been created and easily agreed to.

When it comes to a startup with no history, valuation of the business is a tricky subject. However, as I describe below, that valuation is central to calculating what ownership share is a fair exchange for the investment.

Dilution over the Long Term

At each round of financing, similar calculations are done. So long as the business valuation goes up, and the company does well, dilution of ownership is a bittersweet experience. Continued investment allows the business to grow, but the owner's share of that growth gets smaller. However, with every round of financing and valuation negotiation, things get more complicated, especially if you start a company as a cofounder rather than a sole owner.

Here are the main points to keep in mind:

1. The more partners you bring in at the start, the bigger the dilution downstream. In hindsight, when I started my first company, I really should have gone with convertible notes to forestall valuation, but I had not even heard of such mechanisms back then. Many startups behave like a jolly-boys outing, but consider every

partner carefully. If someone isn't necessary for the growth of the business, can you find other ways to get that starting capital?

2. Time is your enemy. The objective is to grow fast and either succeed alone or get acquired. Because the threats of changing technologies and of competition from abroad are so great in today's world — the average life of a company is a fraction of what it used to be — I believe exiting by being acquired is more attractive as a strategy than it has ever been.

3. The first pre-money valuation is critical (see below). Stand your ground, and use the business-plan process to justify your valuation. Again, in hindsight, I know that my first investor would have accepted the same percentage equity whether I had asked for $2.1 million or a much larger number.

4. Each round of financing adds layers of complexity that can further dilute the ownership of the founders.

Imagine you have a winning idea, but only $50,000 in savings to make it a real success. At that moment you own 100 percent of an idea valued at $50,000, which is equivalent to your working capital (this means the cash available to run the business). You know you need more money to start — let's say $300,000 — so you convince three friends to put in another $50,000 each, from a mixture of savings, credit cards, and loans leveraged against homes. Now the idea's value is $200,000, and you each own 25 percent because you each invested $50,000 of working capital.

That's not enough, though. So you write a business plan that shows investors that, with another $100,000, you can successfully manufacture, market, and sell your product. You convince an angel investor to add $100,000, which raises the valuation of the company to $300,000, (the original $200,000 from the four cofounders plus the angel's $100,000), which at this stage is really just the actual value of all the money put in. Bringing in the external investment immediately dilutes the ownership percentage of you and your three pals.

The angel investment is worth one-third a share of the value ($100,000/$300,000), and the four founders now share equally two-thirds of the company. You each still own $50,000 in equity, but as a percentage of the whole business, your share drops to 16.67 percent each.

You start the company and sales grow to $500,000 a year. Then an opportunity to acquire a competitor suddenly arrives. That needs more cash. With the help of the angel investor, you convince a venture capital fund that your valuation is now three times annual revenue, or $1.5 million (most of the deal offers I have received have been at multiples of three times revenue or seven times net profits). This is called the "pre-money valuation," meaning the value of the company *before* the new money arrives. The venture capital fund agrees to invest another $1.5 million, which raises the "post-money valuation" to $3 million. Your little startup has done well, but you now have to recalculate ownership shares.

In the post-money valuation of your business, the venture capital company immediately owns 50 percent ($1.5 million/$3 million). The remaining 50 percent is split between the founders and the angel investor according to the prior ownership amounts. The angel investor, who had a third of the company prior to the venture capital investment, gets diluted to one-third of the remaining 50 percent, which is 16.67 percent ownership (which is worth $500,000). The angel investor should be happy: They increased their initial investment fivefold.

That leaves 33.33 percent left for the original four pals, which is a dilution to 8.33 percent each. You started out with 100 percent ownership of a winning idea worth $50,000. Now you have only

8.33 percent ownership of the actual business, but that share is worth $249,900 (or 8.33 percent of $3 million). You should also be happy, as your investment increased fivefold.

Let's take things to the next stage. Your decision to bring in venture capital pays off, and your growth is continuous. Annual sales reach $1.5 million a year. After intense negotiations involving lawyers on both sides (lawyers who need to be paid), it is agreed that the company now has a pre-money valuation of $5 million. In other words, if you exited via a sale now, your ownership share of 8.33 percent of $5 million would be worth $416,500 (minus capital gains taxes).

However, you and everyone else want to keep growing. Another opportunity shows up, and everyone agrees to raise a series B round of financing of $5 million. (As a reminder, the "seed round" of financing was the initial $300,000, and the series A round was the additional $1.5 million). Post-money, the company is now worth $10 million (your valuation of $5 million plus the new money).

It is also agreed that the company needs to create a stock option pool to attract top talent to the growing company. In a typical deal, the pre-money team creates that pool from their equity shares. Everyone agrees to allocate 5 percent in total, which dilutes everyone's equity shares by 5 percent. The VC allocates 5 percent of their 50 percent (leaving them 47.5 percent), the angel investor allocates 5 percent of their 16.67 percent (leaving them 15.84 percent), and each of the four founder pals allocates 5 percent of their 8.33 percent (leaving 7.91 percent ownership each).

Of course, your share of 7.91 percent doesn't sound like much, but that means your share of your $10-million company is now $791,000. If, after a few more successful years down the line, everyone agrees to sell the company for $30 million in cash, your share would be $2,373,000.

At the outset you might have refused to give up 33.33 percent to the angel investor, but the money brought in helped you grow. You may all have groaned silently when the VC took 50 percent ownership for $1.5 million. But you have to ask yourself, without any of those additional investments, how far would you have gotten if you tried to build the company with your original $50,000? You might still own 100 percent of $50,000 minus all your expenses, but $2,373,000 is a better outcome.

Part of the Plan:
Calculate Your Business Value

After coming to terms with exchanging ownership for cash investment, the main challenge is establishing and agreeing to the valuation of the startup entity. This is something that you calculate in your business plan, and it's recalculated every time you ask someone to invest more capital in the business. If your business is already generating revenue and profits, it is relatively easy to calculate value by simply comparing your business to similar companies in size and revenue that have recently been purchased by a larger company. Taking all the deals and establishing an average multiple on revenue and/or profit, you can then apply that to your business. The same applies for companies involved in research and development that are pre-revenue.

However, in the example above, when all you have is a winning idea and $50,000 to invest of your own money, then a potential investor will calculate the business valuation at $50,000. If you want someone to invest, say, $100,000, to help fund growth, then that investor will expect a two-thirds ownership share. However, if you are only willing to give up a 25 percent share of ownership, then you are telling the investor that you value your business much higher — since $100,000 would be equivalent to a one-quarter share of ownership only if the post-money valuation was $400,000. The business would have $150,000 in cash to use for working capital, but somehow you are saying that if the business was sold straightaway, it would be worth $400,000.

In this scenario, the question that potential investors will ask is: What is that valuation based on? What, besides your own cash investment, is of value? Do you have customers lined up? Have you contracts in hand? Are strategic company buyers queuing up to get hold of your idea and willing to pay a premium? What preorders can you guarantee? In your business plan, specify whatever you think adds value to justify whatever initial business valuation you decide on. This might be a first-in-class product; it might be that you tested your product using a proof-of-concept beta version and have data that potential customers will purchase it once you have the funds to manufacture it; or perhaps you already moved from idea to some important milestone without having to invest a lot. Each milestone achieved adds value.

Further, once a company has been in business for a year or two, it develops a track record of proven revenue, a customer base, inventory, and so on. These things all add value above and beyond whatever a sole owner's initial cash investment was. Product expansions and upgrades, opening new markets, international sales, and so on, all demonstrate the potential for further growth — and that adds value. In development, hitting key milestones can catapult valuation, since the likelihood of a larger company being willing to buy you for a premium increases.

Of course, you think your company is great, but investors need a degree of confidence that their money is going to bring a return. The less you can guarantee or predict, the more ownership they will want in order to mitigate their risk. In reality, if you have never run a business, and you have little or no money, most investors will want to be majority owners from the start. That is not because they want to steal your idea, but because they have more money at risk.

One way to overcome this issue is to agree to a hybrid deal that starts out with the investor as a majority owner, but this flips as soon as you are able to repay their initial investment. Initial and post-return ownership is subject to negotiation. This is not a common model, and I might be the only one to ever do it this way, but most investors like this idea.

Ultimately, the process of valuation is a negotiation between you as the person with the brilliant idea and the investors who see potential in it. As I note above, valuation gets calculated in two ways: *pre-money* refers to a company's value *before* it receives outside financing, while *post-money* refers to its value *after* outside funds are added. Ownership or equity shares are based on what percentage the outside funds represent of the total post-money valuation.

As another example, suppose that an entrepreneur and an investor both agree that a high-tech startup is worth, pre-money, $500,000. If the investor then provides an additional $250,000, the post-money valuation bumps up to $750,000, and the investor would get a one-third equity share (since $250,000 is one-third of $750,000).

This means that entrepreneurs must fight hard for the best pre-money valuation possible, which adds even more weight to the need to perform the business-plan process with real stakeholder feedback.

The Pitch: Presenting to Investors

If you are seeking investors, then your first goal is to create a thorough, detailed business plan. However, you will also need to pitch your winning idea to investors in person. To do this, you need to create a convincing, concise presentation, one that typically includes a slideshow or a short video. Of course, many people start sweating just thinking about public speaking, and I provide advice about this next. Here are my suggestions for getting that pitch absolutely right.

Keep It Short and Don't Oversell

A mistake many entrepreneurs make is to torture potential investors with a lengthy slideshow. In the book *Brain Rules*, author and development molecular biologist John Medina shares the science of attention and concludes that it is impossible for the brain to concentrate for more than ten minutes. In my experience that is very long for an investor. You need to be able to present your idea in less than five minutes.

Like the elevator pitch (see page 61), this should be a catchy, exciting summary with as much visual stimulation as possible because the brain mostly memorizes through vision. Your objective is to hook someone's interest, so that they hopefully ask for more information. Have your business plan and separate executive summary in hand if they are requested, but don't re-create your business plan in twenty-five slides. My rule is, for the first presentation, use no more than five slides or a five-minute video. Keep in mind that no one in the room will make a decision based on a presentation. If they are intrigued, they'll ask for more detail. They may interrogate you, which is what you want. They may propose bringing in an expert in your area of the business as a follow-up; in fact, if they don't suggest that, you should. Only after they perform due diligence will a decision be made.

To me, the biggest mistake is when a presenter tries to say everything, and more, about the business, the market, and the future. Resist this urge. The more you tell investors at the first presentation, the more reasons you give them to disqualify you and say no to a follow-up meeting. Your objective is purely to get them intrigued.

Be Eye-Catching and Polished

Investors know you are starting out and strapped for cash, but you cannot risk looking amateurish. Your slides or video should not look homemade. Investors are often connected to successful, sophisticated companies who have invested a small fortune on their image and branding. So invest in your own. Use professional editing and great images. This is even more important when you only have a handful of slides or a short video. Have someone else proof the presentation for grammar and typos.

The Perfect Pitch in Five Slides

Here is a template for the perfect pitch. Though I've used slides, follow the same organization in a video.

Slide 1: The Problem or Need

Show the problem you intend to fix or the need your business fills. Make it urgent and dramatic. Hit them with the main message right away. Don't waste their time with introductory slides, agendas, or personal information. They know who you are already and why you are there. Get their attention immediately with a sharp message that reflects the passion that made you mad and want to change the world in the first place.

Slide 2: The Money

Show them the money! Investors love big numbers. Show them the total market and the percentage you believe your company can carve out with your unique solution.

Slide 3: The Business Summary

In two or three bullet points, outline how the business will operate. What and how will you market and sell? What tactics will you use to turn their money into profit for them?

Slide 4: The Entrepreneur

Tell your audience *briefly* about yourself and your core team, such as the inventor, engineer, or scientist who is essential to your success. What qualifies you to execute the plan better than anyone else? Don't provide your biography or résumé, but tell them what, in a nutshell, qualifies you to spend their money wisely. Investors invest in either the horse (the idea for a product or service) or the jockey (the entrepreneur). There are thousands of horses available, but great jockeys are prized.

Slide 5: The Call for Action

As an investor, I shut down if someone makes a great presentation but fails to attempt to close the sale by asking me to do something. If someone doesn't try to get me to take action, then how can I believe that they will get customers to buy their product or service? My call-to-action slide is always the same. It consists of an eye-catching background and two words: NEXT STEPS? While the investors stare at it with a mixture of thoughts in their minds, I will close the sale verbally.

Closing the Sale

I prefer what I call "action closes." These are attempts to get the investor to commit to further action that keeps them interested in what you have to sell. As I say, investors don't make investment decisions at a presentation, but they do decide whether to continue considering the investment. An action close can be as simple as asking for the name of the most appropriate analyst to send the business plan to, but if you can get more specific, it really helps.

Think of it like, "If you eat your vegetables, I'll let you have some ice cream." A solid action close would be to say something like the following:

> If you like the concept of my company, what I would like to do is set up a telephone conference with several potential customers who have said they would be interested in buying product X once I have the $2 million I need to manufacture it. That will give you the chance to quiz them about the market and why we offer advantages over the competition. You can hear it from their perspective rather than mine. I can set up a conference call for Friday. What time works for you?

If people offer "buying signals," or statements of interest or curiosity, respond to these with explanations or other appropriate calls to action, but keep it pertinent. Don't go off on tangents or start generally chatting. Then shut up, especially if they agree to consider the proposal further. Thank them for their consideration and get out.

Above all, *don't linger after the presentation.* Just because everyone is friendly doesn't mean you are now friends. More investments have been lost after the sales pitch than during. Usually the presenter relaxes and says something dumb, which leads to more questions, and that can lead to overselling. And overselling leads to disqualification.

The secret to successful salesmanship in any situation is to close on the buying signal with a call for action, shut up, let them decide, and then thank them and leave. Of course, whatever is said, also follow up later, either in the way that is requested or simply to again express gratitude for their consideration.

Successful Public Speaking: Be Calm and Passionate

From wedding speeches to stage presentations, speaking in public is a top-five cause of stress. Surveys show that 75 percent of people suffer from public-speaking anxiety. People describe increasing symptoms of anxiety before a presentation. The heart starts racing. Breathing becomes shallow. Hands and knees shake. Most often, the reason people feel nervous is because they feel they need to be perfect and that the audience is judging their presentation.

However, to me, when it comes to making presentations to investors, *passion is everything.* To be honest, I am often disappointed when I listen to entrepreneurs pitch their ideas. That's not because presenters are nervous, or because their presentations aren't polished, but because people often don't speak with passion and enthusiasm. I care not if someone is nervous; I have been nervous thousands of times, and I understand what it feels like. Frankly, I expect people to be nervous; I think it is a sign of someone who really wants something. Someone who doesn't care about the outcome doesn't get nervous. What I want to hear in the voice is passion and excitement.

Passion is what got me my first investor. Years later, the investor told me that he initially only agreed to meet with me as a favor for a friend. He intended to send me packing with a lecture about how hard it is to raise money and how I should just get another regular job. However, my passion for the business, and the way it could fix a wrong, kept him listening. It is less about what you say and more about how you say it.

Tips to Calm Nerves

One time, I was with a peer group as we rehearsed our presentations for a coming meeting. The person next to me became so anxious that, when it came her turn to speak, she fainted.

Later, I asked her why she got so nervous. She said that everyone who had gone before her seemed so competent that she became increasingly intimidated. She thought she was the only one in the room who felt nervous and that surely everyone else would notice. She was desperately afraid of looking foolish.

When I described to her my own racing heart, dry mouth, sweating brow, and the fear that I would screw up or that my jokes would fall flat, she was surprised. All she saw was confidence. So I asked her to trust me and to let me video her practicing the talk.

I also taught her a simple calming technique that I have used for years. Do this breathing exercise about ten minutes before your moment in the spotlight. Take deep inhalations and exhalations, making each inhalation and exhalation last about four to six seconds. Push the inhalation down against the diaphragm. Try to focus only on the breath and fill the chest to capacity.

Next I discussed a few body language tips, the same ones others had shared with me. They always work: Begin by standing in what I call the "Wonder Woman pose." This is legs apart, hands defiantly on hips, chest slightly forward, head held high. This stance is clinically proven to change hormone levels, creating confidence and reducing fear. Maintain this pose for ten minutes before any meeting or speech. I even do this when preparing for tricky phone conferences.

The next tip is to use the hands and head to engage with the audience and get them on your side. This is difficult to describe in words, but there are excellent short videos available online (see the endnotes). By keeping our hands in a palm upward position, we engender trust. By turning the head occasionally to look to the farthest reaches of the audience on either side of the room, we engender sincerity.

The woman did this while I recorded her talk on a video camera. Even with just the two of us, and a technician to run the slides on a background screen, she was still nervous, but her breathing was deeper, and I noticed her hands stopped shaking.

When she finished and left the stage, she was almost in tears. In her judgment, she had choked on certain words, her voice had quavered, and she said that we must have seen how much she was shaking.

Then we sat down and watched a video playback. She was stunned to see how confident she looked and how calm her voice was through the whole presentation. On the recording, she looked poised.

The next day she was no less nervous, but I coached her through the breathing technique again, and she automatically took on the Wonder Woman pose. On stage, she came over as totally confident and received a thunderous round of applause. Afterward, she sent me a note:

> I wanted to let you know how things went for me inside my head. In a nutshell, WONDERFUL!! Between spending some time onstage prior to the event (to get comfortable with my surroundings and how I would stand, where the screen was, etc.), and the breathing technique, and doing a Wonder Woman impression, it was surprisingly less stressful than I could have ever imagined. I even started to enjoy myself up there.

CHAPTER SIX

A Virtual Business

Build the Hub

If you deprive yourself of outsourcing, and your competitors do not, you're putting yourself out of business.

— Lee Kuan Yew

The shift from the industrial age to the information age is causing one of the most disruptive eras the business world has ever experienced…and in my opinion, that is a great thing. The same changes in information systems and technology that are disrupting and causing the downfall of once-untouchable conglomerates offer significant advantages to startup companies and provide an unprecedented opportunity for you to gain financial independence through your own venture, whether in commerce or arts. They allow startups to be structured in a totally original way. I call this the "hub" model, though it's also known somewhat disparagingly as a "virtual business."

In other words, instead of doing what 96 percent of traditional startups do — leasing an office, hiring staff, and mimicking the hierarchical structure of large corporations — my advice is to take a contrarian approach and do the opposite: Hire no one and work from home as a single entrepreneur who outsources all of the business's necessary functions, including manufacturing, distribution, marketing, financial services, and so on.

I believe that the hub or a quasi-hub model is fundamental for the early survival of startups, especially during the first years when capital is tight, cash flow is critical, expenses are highest, and revenues are lowest. I am not saying that a hub structure is best in every situation, since every startup has different needs. In addition, as companies grow, they often need to adjust their structure and become less "virtual." However, the hub model offers a variety of benefits that can help any company, even traditionally structured corporations, be more nimble and flexible, and in the formative years of a startup, a virtual structure offers advantages that can make the difference between failure and survival.

I've used this model to start all of my companies, and it was so successful and profitable that I never changed the structure before they were sold. I consider it so important to survival I've devoted this entire chapter to it. First, I define the hub model and discuss the downside for startups of traditional company structures and hiring practices. Then I discuss how cross-training helps you, the entrepreneur, succeed at the hub model, along with the advantages of contractors and how to hire them. Finally, I summarize the advantages of not leasing office space and offer my strategies for successfully working from home.

What Is a Hub?

As I say, the hub business model is similar to the virtual business model, but these days the term *virtual business* can conjure negative images of mom-and-pop companies or fly-by-night internet entities. So I prefer the term *the hub* because it avoids those negative associations, and also because it clearly describes the model's structure: The owner sits in the middle, and everyone else involved in the business connects directly to that person like spokes on a wheel. Though members are geographically apart, they work together using email and communications technology, and they appear to customers and clients as a single, unified organization with a real physical location. Yet the hub structure requires no hierarchy, and no bricks and mortar, and it avoids the corporate tendency toward meeting madness and wastefulness.

Most large businesses and corporations have departments organized by function, like accounting and finance, administration, legal, information technology, manufacturing and distribution, purchasing and warehousing, sales and marketing, human resources, and so on. Some might have research and development or quality-assurance departments. But a startup often doesn't need to create departments. Instead, every function of a company can be provided by specialist vendors under contract on an as-needed basis, and this can be done at a fraction of the cost and risk it would take to build the same capabilities from scratch. Plus, it's relatively easy to hire a manufacturer, distributor, and accounting firm because so many companies compete to provide those functions. To use another analogy, the hub business model means that you as CEO behave like the conductor of an orchestra, selecting the best players and directing them in harmony.

My companies have all been structured this way. For each, the corporate HQ address has been a mail- and message-forwarding service that costs only a few hundred dollars per quarter. My office is a converted room in my house in Seattle. My accounting firm is located in Dallas. Depending on the company, I have used a network of East Coast companies and consultants, paid on a project-by-project basis, to provide sales and marketing services. For technical and regulatory services, I have used a company based in Canada. A company in San Diego and another in Ohio have handled manufacturing on a project basis, and I have hired an expert consultant from the Midwest for a few hours a week to oversee them. I have contracted services in China and Hong Kong.

I have never hired a full-time or part-time employee or assistant. For the most part, everyone involved in my companies has communicated for free over the internet, and it's always run like a well-oiled clock. Not only that, net profits have typically been around 75 percent.

When I walk into a large company or corporation, I see many instances in which adopting a quasi-virtual structure would save costs and increase revenue and profit. However, it would be almost impossible to take an established, structured company and deconstruct it until the only remaining employee was the owner/manager. With a startup company, however, the opportunity exists to adopt the hub structure and maintain it indefinitely — that is, until that structure is no longer the most effective and efficient for your business.

The hub structure offers startups at least five significant advantages:

1. Like the conductor of an orchestra, the entrepreneur gets to connect and communicate with every function of the business in real-time. Information is unfiltered by layers of managers, which means the owner remains closer to the realities of the market and the customer. Bad news is never filtered out, and decisions can be made instantaneously without the need for formal meetings.

2. No time has to be spent on managing employees, since

there aren't any. The daily management of tasks, projects, and people are handled by each vendor's own internal systems, which frees the startup entrepreneur to focus on their company's growth.

3. Cash is not invested in infrastructure or in hiring people, which both entail high costs. This improves cash flow and frees the entrepreneur to focus on funding the business itself, like with marketing, rather than maintaining an office and paying employee benefits.

4. The entrepreneur can titrate services according to demand and budget, cutting back when demand drops, increasing when demand picks up. This extends survival time and helps the entrepreneur bypass any cash-flow traps.

5. However, one of the biggest advantages to me is the improved quality of my work life! For instance, once the hub structure is in place — once vendors are selected and set up — there is very little for the entrepreneur to do. All the daily tasks take place off-site and out of sight, and contractors only need periodic updates. With my companies, the first six months were the busiest, but even then I didn't work more than five hours a day. That five hours was intense at times, but there really was no need to spend any more time in the office.

The Pros and (Mostly) Cons of Employees

Many first-time entrepreneurs, especially if they come from the corporate world, have a hard time imagining a new company without any employees, so I want to expand on some of these issues as they relate to startups. Experts argue over the pros and cons of outsourcing versus hiring your own staff, but most arguments focus on skills and costs. However, for startups, employees cause the business owner to focus internally at the very time they should be focusing on customers and growth. Employees need to be hired and paid, they need to be managed, and they may not like the "all hands on deck" commitment of a startup. In the early survival phase, that can be catastrophic.

Hiring Employees Can Be Complicated and Expensive

Just one glance at what a diligent business owner must do when they hire their first employees should be enough to convince you that there are better ways to spend your time and money:

1. Obtain an employer identification number.
2. Register with your state's labor department.
3. Get workers' compensation insurance.
4. Set up a payroll system to withhold taxes.
5. Have each employee fill out IRS form W-4, or their withholding allowance.
6. For each new employee, fill out IRS form I-9, or employment eligibility verification.
7. Report each new employee to your state's new-hire reporting agency.
8. Post required notices.
9. File IRS form 940 each year and pay your federal unemployment tax.
10. Adopt workplace safety measures.
11. Create an employee handbook.
12. Set up personnel files.
13. Set up employee benefits.

A regular employee benefits package often includes health-care coverage, retirement plans, travel expenses, paid vacation time, short- and long-term disability insurance coverage, and life insurance. Small businesses aren't required to provide all of these things, and when they do, a startup might ask employees to contribute a percentage of their costs. Then again, these are the types of benefits that many larger corporations use to recruit and retain the best talent, and it may be what your employees want and expect. Many startup entrepreneurs fail to account for the cost of these benefits — whether to replace them for themselves once they leave their current jobs or to provide them for employees they must hire — when they make their business plan, so account for them if you will be hiring staff.

But if you don't absolutely need employees, then consider all of the other more productive things you could be spending your time and money on.

Employees Require Management, Which Means Meetings

When I reflect on my previous career in traditionally structured organizations, I estimate that I spent 75 percent of my time sitting in meetings. Rarely was the topic of the meeting about profitability, cost efficiency, or customer satisfaction. Most meetings were about internal matters like employee morale, human resource systems, and company regulations.

In fact, meetings have increasingly become a great enemy to everyone in corporate America. It is estimated that there are more than eleven million formal meetings per day in the United States alone, and based on my experience, I'd say that most employees consider these meetings a waste of time. On average, each US employee spends over forty hours per month attending meetings, and that does not take into account the even longer time most employees spend to prepare for meetings. It also does not take into account the amount of time people spend in ad hoc meetings in the corridors, by the watercooler or coffeepot, or even in the parking lot.

While a small business with minimal staff may require fewer meetings, those employees and the company's organization still require managing. What the hub structure does is eliminate any need for staff management, which provides the entrepreneur with more time to focus on the business itself — perhaps up to forty more hours a month. Not only that, but the lack of distractions means entrepreneurs can work more efficiently; they can start and complete projects without interruption and achieve more in a fraction of the normal work time. This is why I have been able to achieve in a five-hour workday the same productivity that used to take twelve hours as a corporate employee.

Another, related management issue is workflow. That is, when you start your company, it can be impossible to predict workflow. On slow days or weeks, you may spend most of your time trying to find something productive for your employees to do so that you aren't paying them to stand around twiddling their thumbs. That's a waste of your time and money. Even in well-managed, cash-rich companies, I can often make a case for downsizing because so many employees do not contribute to profitability.

Startups Can Be a Culture Shock

It's no surprise, and it's even expected, that the first concern of most employees is their job and personal circumstances. Their first loyalty is to themselves, not to the company or its customers. This is why, in order to attract and retain the best employees, most large companies offer a variety of benefits, competitive compensation, and lots of perks and individual attention.

However, an entrepreneur is the opposite. All of their work time, energy, and financial resources are being put into the startup, and entrepreneurs need employees or contractors who are willing to work hard and well and with minimal supervision, and who are also willing to make their own sacrifices, as necessary, on behalf of the business. That is just the nature of the startup world. Compensation might be less, flexibility will be necessary, responsibilities might change, and pay raises might not happen regularly. In a startup, everyone must be in it together, builders all.

Many corporate employees are attracted to the lure of a startup. They have watched the rise of Facebook and Google and want to be part of a similar rocket ride to riches. That's not the reality for most startups. Startups are rarely stable. Half of all startups fail. And startup employees need to think and act like owners: doing both the job they were hired for and anything else that's needed, such as cleaning the floors and emptying the trash cans, without being asked. That can be a culture shock for many corporate or career employees who jump from the security of the corporate world into the fly-by-the-seat-of-your-pants culture of a startup. It takes a particular kind of person and mindset to flourish in this situation.

For instance, a friend of mine joined a startup. Over beers for the next twelve months, I got to hear an all-too-common tale of woe. The CEO had a great idea, but he had no sense of how to run a startup. Instead, he replicated the corporate world he was trained in. He hired someone to be the sales and marketing expert, another person to be the software expert, another to be the procurer of the hardware, and two others. All the employees were plucked from stable corporate jobs. With six full-time employees — in addition to the salary the CEO paid himself — their seed capital was used up quickly. Eventually, the sales expert got the first order, but it was for a product and service that the software engineer said could not be fulfilled. However, the hardware expert went ahead and procured the parts, which remain unused, since a final product never materialized.

This farcical process was repeated a few times until the sales expert left for a better-paying job. The CEO immediately hired a replacement, but then the hardware expert made an ultimatum to the CEO: If he did not get a significant pay raise and more stock options, he would leave. He even suggested that budget be freed up by firing the new sales guy.

The sales expert saved himself by finding another customer for a product they were able to make, but the company wanted to charge a ridiculous price in order to cover the costs of all their other failures to date. The customer balked.

Thus, today, the CEO spends all his time trying to raise more capital and placate his staff, who murmur in open rebellion all day long. Don't let this happen to you. Avoid hiring employees as long as possible, and ideally only once your company is more stable. But if you must hire employees, look for those who understand what life in a startup really means.

A Virtual Business Means Rethinking Company Structure

Organizational structure is a complex topic, one that's more pertinent to larger companies. However, startup entrepreneurs need to strategize and explain their company structure when drafting their business plan. This means deciding whether to go hub or quasi-hub, and if you'll be hiring employees, in what capacities and in what type of organization. For entrepreneurs who are coming from large companies or corporations, this may mean unlearning a particular culture of communication and decision-making. This is because one of the biggest advantages of a startup is its lack of bureaucracy. The hub model allows for speedy decision-making as well as strategic flexibility. Many new business owners, however, rush to replicate the levels of corporate management they are familiar with, thereby diluting this advantage.

The traditional organizational structure employs a familiar power dynamic in which somebody leads, extra managers deputize, and the rest follow. This is similar to a military style of leadership. Decisions are made at the top, and the organization has control and stability. Although quite common, this type of structure is risky in markets where technology changes rapidly. It takes a long time for information to get from the field at the bottom of the pyramid to the decision makers at the top, and it can take just as long for a decision to filter back down to be implemented.

Other structures attempt to delegate decision-making to project teams, functions, or divisions, but the challenge here is that those segments tend to then form a traditional structure within themselves. The function or project team can form a fiefdom, with their goals taking priority over the corporate strategy.

For a startup, function leaders are an expensive hire, and they usually want to hire underlings quickly, partly to cement their positional power and partly to delegate the tasks they don't enjoy doing. I often joke that the smaller the company, the bigger the job title of the employees. It is common to find a startup that boasts a CEO, COO, and an executive team of VPs organized by function or project. The VPs hire directors. The directors hire associate directors. The associates hire managers. And in no time, not only has a huge amount of cash been drained, but a complicated decision tree is put in place.

Even in a "lean" company, with relatively few hires, the decision-making process tends to mirror the traditional structure, which defaults to decision-making by consensus, mistaking this for a democratic process. A truly democratic process means the most votes win. Consensus is a form of reverse dictatorship: No one leaves the room until everyone agrees, and typically that will be when everyone agrees with the boss!

Whether a startup has a traditional structure or is "flatter," with teams that each report to the owner, a lot of time will be spent reaching consensus. And that's probably the greatest cost of all these structures: lost time waiting for decisions to get made.

This is also the great advantage of the hub model for startups, especially in the early years. Entrepreneurs can make decisions quickly and change those decisions just as fast. What the hub model requires, though, is flexibility and multitasking, which is a way of working that is not cultivated in corporate America. Many people, especially men, can have a hard time with it. This is another reason I suggest taking quiet time and reconnecting in nature (see pages 17–21), since these help rewire the brain to a new way of thinking. Multitasking reflects the power of the feminine, and if I can learn to do it, anyone can, since prior to making those activities daily habits, I was purely a one-task-at-a-time person.

Corporate America: Slow and Inflexible

According to Professor Richard Foster from Yale University, the average life expectancy for a large company has decreased from sixty-seven years in the 1920s to fifteen years today. Half of the once-untouchable major airlines filed for chapter 11 bankruptcy protections in the early 2000s, and American car makers such as Ford, GM, and Chrysler had to be bailed out by billions of taxpayer dollars.

All those companies and more have issued a plethora of

reasons for their struggles and demises. In part, the shift from regional to global markets has led to an increase in mergers and acquisitions, as well as to an increase in competition from around the world. Rising fuel costs, cheaper, better-made imports, and difficult economic times have all certainly played a role. But to me, the difficulties facing corporations can all be distilled to one overarching thing: Their management structures are too inefficient to react to change fast enough. As for GM, a *USA Today* story reported:

> In an early 2006 speech, [GM billionaire investor Kirk Kerkorian] spelled out what he thought GM needed to do to right itself: Be more realistic about market share and revenue expectations, cut excess products and brands, sell or close business units that weren't making money, and take what he called a "clean sheet of paper approach to the business," looking at everything in the company with fresh eyes. Most important, all of it needed to be done fast. "Time is of the essence," he said.

Management, however, simply could not change fast enough to follow his advice.

Since these seismic company crashes, many experts have preached the benefits of lean companies. Lean, however, has not necessarily meant fewer people or less investment in infrastructure. Lean aims for more efficient communication and quicker decision-making in markets that can change dramatically with each upgrade in technology, but it still requires cash investment in infrastructure and people. Replacing vertically aligned teams with horizontally aligned teams does result in speedier decisions, but it still costs a lot and takes time to build and run.

One positive example is Amazon, which is the largest internet retailer and which has used a largely virtual structure to define its strategy. Amazon is mostly a mass of web pages and computer servers, but of course it has a distribution network, thousands of staff, and inventory. Yet it externalizes or outsources all its nonessential activities, which allows Amazon to be more responsive and to adapt and adjust based on the market and competition. Even large, previously inflexible companies such as IBM, Hewlett Packard, AT&T, and GM have recently attempted to become more agile by introducing more quasi-virtual structures. The old organizational model — based on large groups of people doing specialized tasks with centralized coordination — is evolving to meet the rapid changes in the global marketplace. However, with the right preparation and mindset, entrepreneurs can run their startups in the most efficient and nimble way from the beginning.

Ditch the Mastermind Principle

Another reason that many new business owners spend their first few months hiring function leaders — like a head of finance, a COO, a human resources manager, and so on — is because they only have expertise in one function of the business, like finance, design, or marketing. If, in their previous career, an entrepreneur never got to learn other functions and other areas, they can lack that all-important ingredient: self-confidence.

Shortly before writing this book, I was invited to give a talk to a group of first-time CEOs. I asked them what was the first thing they did when they started, and all the startup CEOs said they hired people to lead various functions in the company, though sometimes their investors made the hires for them. Though this hiring was expensive and sucked millions out of the cash reserves of their companies, these CEOs were happy to have experienced people they trusted alongside. They said things like, "I came into the job through marketing and don't know the rest of the business," or "Human resources is such a specialized field these days." Then one CEO chirped, "It is the mastermind principle," and heads around the room nodded in support.

The mastermind principle is at the core of a famous self-help book by Napoleon Hill, a man who failed at over twenty ventures, never succeeded in building a successful business, and whose own son labeled him a charlatan. Nevertheless, his book *Think and Grow Rich* has sold tens of millions of copies since its publication in 1937.

Hill's life story should be enough for anyone to discount his observations of what it takes to grow rich, but still today, blogs and business magazine articles sometimes bestow a saint-like quality on him and extol the virtues of the mastermind principle. Hill attributed the concept to Andrew Carnegie, the steel tycoon who died in 1919, a full eighteen years before Hill's observations were published. It was claimed that Carnegie attributed his wealth and success to surrounding himself with a "group of men of brains," tapping into their ideas and some sort of extra psychic bonus that such a group created. In business today, the concept has been taken to mean a leader being surrounded by a group of experts, all aspiring for a common goal, and this principle has directly or indirectly influenced the way most companies and their management teams have been structured.

Of course, Carnegie was no longer around to confirm or deny Hill's interpretation of his leadership style, but I take a different, almost opposite lesson from Carnegie's life. Carnegie had no tolerance for sycophants, and his circle of leaders was in fact not composed of "function experts." They were self-sufficient CEOs who each knew every function of their businesses intimately, and Carnegie was no different.

Carnegie learned the principles of the manufacturing function from his youthful days as a bobbin boy in a textile factory. He was thirsty for knowledge and took an interest in all aspects of manufacturing, beyond the limited boundary of his job. Then, being one of the few educated workers, he was promoted to a clerk in the accounting department. Here he learned the art of bookkeeping as well as the challenges of cash-flow management.

With the invention of the telegraph, Carnegie eventually got a job as a messenger. Rather than deliver messages to people's residences, he worked out more efficient distribution routes and delivered messages directly to people when they were at work or in the marketplace. Satisfied recipients were good tippers and liked to keep the same messenger. He took away from the experience the importance of good customer service for repeat orders.

Later in the railroad business he used the same principles of efficient distribution to create more cost-effective ways to clear up accidents and keep stock rolling. It served him tremendously as an industrialist, when resourceful distribution of materials during a recession became crucial for profits.

With money in his pocket, Carnegie became an investor, first in a railroad, and then in oil exploration. He helped build companies that made railroad bridges and rolling stock. After visiting steel plants in Sheffield, England, he returned to America rightly convinced that steel would eventually replace iron as the construction material of choice. He started his first steel plant in 1875.

Throughout his career, Carnegie armed himself with enough information of every function in a business to be able to judge what the people around him were recommending, to foresee issues before they arose, and to see opportunities that others could not perceive. He was able to make decisions for every function, and many times those went against the common thinking. In other words, to me, the lesson of Carnegie's success is not to surround yourself with experts, but to become an expert yourself in as many functions as possible.

Part of the Plan:
Get Cross-Function Experience

For the entrepreneur, what this means is, the more cross-function experience you can get before starting your business, the greater your knowledge and self-confidence will be, and the less need you will have to hire function leaders or employees. The cash benefit is obvious, but you will also be able to make quicker, more-intuitive decisions. That is critical in the early, bumpy phase of a startup. This same awareness and self-confidence is also developed through meditation and nature immersion. Of course, it's ideal, like Carnegie, to have direct experience working in a variety of business functions, but we can also glean valuable lessons and understandings simply by paying attention. I have never viewed business and mindfulness as mutually exclusive. Quite the opposite.

Before I started my first company, and like many first-time entrepreneurs, I had expertise only in a single business function. I started in sales. Those readers who work in sales might claim there is a skill involved, and if there is, then in my opinion, it is one that anyone can learn. You talk to customers, listen to what they tell you, and find some way to satisfy their need.

Other aspects of the business, however, fascinated me. Whenever I had the opportunity to talk with people from those other functions, such as manufacturing or finance, I would jump at it. People love to talk about what they do, and I always asked them to identify the key aspects of their role and the biggest challenges and risks they faced. Everyone was keen to take me on a tour of his or her department, and sometimes I was invited to sit in at meetings. I would repeat this "shadowing" activity several times a year and with different people in each function.

These conversations led to a better understanding of how the different functions worked together in a company and how decisions in one area impacted the other functions. It was easier to see how poor communication across functions caused issues and how the traditional company hierarchical structure slowed the decision-making process.

I noticed how much everyone filtered the information that they passed along to their supervisors and how afraid they were to share bad news or information about risks and threats. By the time a situation report ended up on the desk of a CEO, it bore little resemblance to the reality of the event that triggered its production.

Years later, I was fortunate to be hired by a CEO who was passionate about cross-function experience. The head of marketing had previously been the chief financial officer. The heads of manufacturing and distribution had swapped roles. The leader of human resources had formerly been a sales manager. To traditionalists, it probably seemed crazy, but the company became a big success and the CEO was a darling of Wall Street. I recall the marketing manager confessing that he feared being caught out as a fraud because, he said, "I have no training, and I don't know what I am doing." In my opinion he was the best marketing leader I had ever worked for, and I think one of the reasons was that he had no preconceived notion of how things should be done. Everything was freshly questioned.

Throughout my early career, I also got to work in functions for which I had no formal training. I found that the fundamentals of leadership in every function are pretty much the same, which is the ability to manage and direct a small group of people. So when it came time to start my own company, I had a high level of self-confidence, since I had at least some knowledge and experience in every function. I never felt the need to hire function experts. Instead I hired part-time consultants and let them get on with their jobs without onerous updates and reporting requirements. I knew I could spot issues or opportunities when they came up and not be blindsided through ignorance of the function.

This is what I suggest that all startup entrepreneurs do: Arm yourself with sufficient knowledge to run a business without feeling the need to hire function leaders. If possible, do this before launching your business, so that you can incorporate any new understandings and expertise in your business plan. Yet it's never too late to learn. We live in a marvelous age in which technology, transport, and communication systems mean you don't have to work your way through every department to get knowledge, although if you don't plan to start a company for a few years, it's something to consider. However, here are three things you can do anytime to gain knowledge and self-confidence.

Shadow Function Leaders

What's called a *preceptorship* is a period of observational training that's often used for future medical professionals. A more-experienced medical professional (or preceptor) provides observation time for the less-experienced person. It works just as well in business, but it is rarely used. In my regular career I did as much of this as time allowed. Although you can't learn the intricacies of accounting just by watching a CFO at work, you can learn the bigger picture quite easily. You can see how different parts of the business impact cash flow and learn the challenges of balancing revenues with profit and income.

If you have never made sales calls before or understood marketing, or you feel intimidated by both, you should spend a few days in the field with some sales representatives. They are usually glad of the company. It is a great way to learn tips for cold calling, overcoming objections, and closing the sale. It will raise self-confidence in your ability to interact with customers. Similarly, you can attend manufacturing audits and simply watch and learn. By doing preceptorships in this way, you get many real-life insights that cannot be learned in a classroom.

Shadowing function leaders for a day also provides what I call the "Wizard of Oz benefit." That is, you pull back the curtain to reveal the true nature of what people do, and you oftentimes realize you already possess the ability and smarts to do it as well. In *The Wizard of Oz*, Dorothy thinks she needs the "great and powerful Oz" to get home, but Oz is a conman, not a wizard. Instead, Dorothy learns that, all along, she has had the power to get home by herself.

Attend Seminars and Conferences

Another way to gain cross-function knowledge and self-confidence is to attend a seminar that focuses on whatever business function you need more experience in. Every year, there are hundreds of events on finance, research, regulations, marketing, and manufacturing. If you are still working a regular job, plan to attend a conference on each major business function this next year. More than likely, there are plenty of such activities in your local area; search online to find them. Attend lectures to help identify the key issues in today's market.

An added benefit is meeting people who work in that

function. By listening to them, you will learn how they speak and understand any insider acronyms and jargon. You can also make contacts and develop relationships that you can call on later for advice or help.

Take Online Business Courses

Technology gives you access to an array of business courses online, many of which focus on providing cross-function education. There are many local courses you can find that will broaden your awareness. Getting a full-blown MBA is not necessary to run a startup, but if you decide to complete an MBA course, keep in mind that most curricula are designed to improve middle-management skill sets. They teach human resource skills, management by objectives, project leadership, and classic marketing tactics. Much of that isn't useful for a startup that does not have a product or single client yet. Hand on heart, I can say for myself that I cannot think of a single technique that was taught in my MBA that I use in the startup phase. If you want to take classes, my advice is to look for courses that teach the rudiments of different functions.

Staff the Hub:
The Advantages of Outsourcing

I have already mentioned some of the advantages of using the hub model and outsourcing, but perhaps the biggest is the impact on your customers. Customers have a right to expect the same quality of service from every function of your business as they do from an established multinational firm. They are under no obligation to show empathy simply because you are a startup, and no business can excuse poor levels of service just because they are new or small. Outsourcing functions to expert providers means the customer immediately experiences the same high level of service with your fledgling company as they do with a large, established one. Satisfied customers always return and refer others. Dissatisfied customers rarely return, and they turn off others.

Here are some of the other benefits of outsourcing, which is also a list of the qualities that you, as CEO, are looking for in a vendor. Make sure everyone you contract with has a positive track record for and promises all of these benefits.

- **Serving your business is the vendor's priority:** Vendors have to perform well or you will not retain them or use them in the future. Therefore, they have a built-in motivation to work hard, do well, and provide value for money. Contractor attitude is typically: "What can I do for you and your company?" There is no "employee entitlement attitude" to deal with. They are already owners of a small business, so they understand what you are going through. In fact, they hope your business will grow, since that will increase their own business if you continue to hire them, and they can offer valuable advice and resources, such as networks of other experts, beyond the job they have been hired to do.

- **Customers won't know that vendors are not your company:** Outsource providers adopt your company name when they interact with customers, so you will always give the impression to customers and clients of being a bigger company. I have used one outsource vendor that services over 150 businesses ranging in size from a sole proprietor to a multinational. My company was a modest revenue generator for them. Regardless, when any customer called the dedicated toll-free phone number provided by the vendor, they would hear the correct company name and be treated to the same quality as the multinational.

- **You hire expertise rather than train employees:** Vendors are usually experts at their jobs with excellent reputations, their business depends on keeping up with industry standards, and they obviously have the confidence to work unsupervised. To hire employees with that amount of expertise and self-assurance would be expensive, and training people while starting a company takes time and energy you don't have.

- **You avoid employee expenses:** As I say, without employees, you avoid all the expenses and regulations that come with them, like providing health insurance and worker's compensation. Finally, vendors come with no tax consequences or administration costs, since vendors are a direct expense that's deductible on your income-tax return as "professional services."

- **Vendors manage themselves:** Working with vendors is simple: You give them a task. They do it. You pay them. Vendors don't need office space; they have their own. They hire, train, and manage their own employees, using their own human resources and performance and appraisal systems. Meetings can be held over the phone or by video conference, and your relationship with them is more of a collaboration than a reporting hierarchy. You don't have to create operating procedures from scratch; vendors usually have template contracts and confidentiality agreements that you can edit as needed. By outsourcing to experienced staff, you can focus your time and energy on business growth.

- **You contract only the services you need:** Vendors typically offer a menu of services, so you can cherry-pick what you want when you need it. You can start with the basics, and add and upgrade as you grow. Outsource contracts allow you the flexibility to add on or cut back services and volume according to demand, which helps cash-flow management. When cash flow is turbulent, being able to pull in the reins of certain functions or to put projects on hold is tremendously helpful to managing money. As CEO, you are looking for a vendor that understands the turbulence of a startup company and that offers flexibility in terms and fees matched to volume. Finally, if things don't work out, letting contractors go is a simple matter of not renewing the contract. Letting employees go is complex, stressful, and expensive.

Hiring Vendors and Contractors

With all that said, one thing should be obvious: When using the hub model, vendor selection is critical. You want people and companies that get on with the job with the minimum of direction from you, so that you can get on with the task of being a successful entrepreneur. This requires trust, since the hub model means allowing others to perform their roles somewhat freely and out of your sight. For micromanager types, this can be a challenge.

One thing that helps is to assess each vendor carefully and thoroughly before signing a contract, in exactly the same way you'd review the qualifications and temperament of a new employee. It is important to assess the knowledge level of the people who will represent your company, to check their references, and to use your intuition. Vendors need to be qualified, but you also need to feel comfortable with the relationship. Ideally, vendors will have lots of successful, happy clients who have already done their due diligence and will share their experiences with you. In addition, one big issue with vendors can be their rate of staff turnover, so ask about this. During the selection process, I always take a guided tour of the vendor facility. This allows me plenty of opportunities to get one-on-one with employees and ascertain what they think of the company and their level of satisfaction.

However, the evaluation phase aside, the process for outsourcing is remarkably simple. You decide what you need, you search for qualified vendors (online or via your network), then you pick up the phone and call them. What could be simpler? For common functions like bookkeeping and accounting, there are typically hundreds of companies to choose from. Other vendors for more specialized functions might take a little more effort to track down, but the process is basically the same.

I prefer to select smaller vendors simply because being a small fish in a small pond is preferable to being a small fish in a big pond. My business is likely to be more important to the smaller vendor, and I get more attention that way. If they are able to offer a good price to a small business and help me grow, it will look great for them in the future. They will always be able to promote the fact that *we were there when he was little more than an idea…and now look where we helped him get!*

Once a general verbal agreement is reached, and you've evaluated the vendor and decided to work with them, you need to finalize terms and sign a contract. Below, I review what goes into a typical contract, along with some of the legal issues with contractors, and offer my advice for how to negotiate terms.

Typical Elements of an Outsourcing Contract

A vendor contract covers every aspect of your business relationship, but perhaps the most important issue is payment terms.

An ideal contract would include a fixed monthly management fee that covers administration costs at the vendor's end, and then everything else would be based on volume pricing. That gives your company the flexibility it needs to manage cash flow by spending only based on activity. Then, when possible, negotiate the longest payment terms you can — typically in sixty or ninety days. Vendors should be empathetic to your need to manage cash flow; after all, they are small businesses, too. If they have stricter repayment terms, ask them for a twelve-month exception, so you can have time to build up revenue and to allow startup costs to flow through. I've even found some suppliers who were willing to allow a payment-free period at the beginning.

Whether it is accounting, manufacturing, or commercialization, I have found all vendors willing to work out a deal. They exist in competitive fields, typically rely on small margins, and are usually keen for the business. They also know that your company might be a great success one day, and this would be a mutual long-term benefit for you both.

Here are the main elements of an outsourcing contract:

- Scope of services clearly laid out in detail.
- Their management fee. This is typically a nominal amount that covers the person-hours of the account manager on the vendor side. You can usually add a fee-free period of, say, six months.
- A one-time setup fee that covers the vendor's administration costs.
- A fee-for-service arrangement for the scope of services provided, for which the vendor bills monthly or quarterly. In this part, you can consider volume discounts or volume incentives that lower unit costs over time.
- The length of the contract. How long depends on how you feel about the vendor. Starting out, it is better to

go for a short-term deal (one to two years) that's automatically renewable. When you feel the relationship is working well, you can go back to the vendor and extend for a longer term, like five years.

- The period of time for notice of cancellation. It's important to agree to a lengthy period, since you will need time to find an alternative vendor if either side does not want to continue the relationship.
- I suggest requesting formal business review periods if these aren't automatically included. Make these quarterly for the first year and annually thereafter. These can be by phone, but having them in the contract guarantees you get the vendor's regular attention.
- Confidentiality clauses ensure the vendor can't reveal the secrets of your winning idea or directly compete with it.

A Legal Word on Consultants

When you outsource functions using the hub model, it's important to understand the legal difference between a contractor or consultant and an employee. Particularly today, when both consultants and employees can telecommute and work from home, the distinction can get blurred, and yet there are significant consequences, in the form of back taxes and penalties, if the IRS audits your business and decides that your "contractors" should in fact be reclassified as "employees." Indeed, some unscrupulous companies misclassify employees as contractors in order to avoid having to pay unemployment, social security, state employment taxes, and Medicare.

To tell whether someone can be classified as a contractor, download the IRS publication 15-A, "Employer's Supplemental Tax Guide" (available at www.irs.gov/pub/irs-pdf/p15a.pdf). In general, a consultant or contractor is someone who has their own business and more than just your company as a client. In other words, they control their work schedule. If you hire someone for a specific short-term project, they would not be classified as an employee, but if you hire a long-term consultant for, say, three days a week on an ongoing basis, some states would classify them as an employee, especially if they only work for you.

Staying on the right side of the law is another reason to ensure you have a written contract with all vendors. Don't rely on a handshake, and be aware that the IRS does perform company audits.

Negotiating with Vendors and Suppliers

Negotiating contracts with vendors might be a new experience for you. However, as the entrepreneur of a startup, this is now part of your job description. You are now chief negotiator and head attorney in your business.

I meet some people who have an inbuilt fear of negotiating. One reason is the psychological fear of being disliked or rejected, but negotiating is an easy thing to learn. Another reason for the fear of negotiating is that an army of experts makes it seem much more difficult than it really is. They often give the impression that negotiating is like a battle to the death.

Others bang on about trying to arrive at a win-win scenario. The goal when starting out, however, is *not* to get the best contract terms, or even a win-win, but to hire the best vendor. What does it benefit you if the one vendor who could help you become a success walks away because you were so intent on negotiating the "best terms" or a win-win? Running a startup is not about winning a negotiation; it is about survival.

In my opinion, negotiating is an easy practice that some

people make difficult when they let their egos rule over their brains. I have had the misfortune to work with a few people who are such pathological negotiators that they have even negotiated their own payoff down just to feed their insane need to negotiate.

I don't know if I am a good or poor negotiator. I know I am not tough, but I also know I keep a clear view of the future aim. To me, that's just common sense. A new, small startup is not worth a lot of profit to a vendor, at least not right away, and burdening them with complicated contracts and attorney wordsmith games can result in them deciding that your business is not worth the legal cost or effort. I have seen that happen many times.

At this stage of the game, I think it is far more important to get the right vendor than to secure the best price. Further, most vendors will have already gone through exhaustive negotiations with larger clients that involved an army of highly paid attorneys. If the template contract a vendor gives you is the same one that a large company has already agreed to, there is a high likelihood that it is strong and fair enough for your company. Why mess with it? If you ask an attorney to review it, you can be guaranteed that the attorney will find things to change. That is how contract attorneys make money. Attorneys everywhere will be incandescent with rage by this advice, but in this situation, I would be an arrogant fool to think I could alter such an already-vetted contract in a meaningful way.

Sometimes, I have done little more than redact the contracts by changing names and addresses. The vendors appreciate the inherent trust I have in them and that our contracts are turned around quickly. Of course, read contracts carefully, but avoid getting into protracted negotiations over small issues. As an entrepreneur, time is your enemy. Your main goal is to get the vendors you need and start running your business.

Also, be aware of the very natural human reaction to negotiating. Rarely will one person propose something without the opposing person countering. It is our nature. In fact, most negotiating skills classes teach that behavior. They say never agree to a proposal without attaching a concession. In other words, say something like, "We can agree to the 10 percent discount on the condition that you agree to [fill in the blank]." That is all well and good in the regular corporate world, but it can be death for the small business. Vendors have neither the time nor patience to dally with a startup they see as playing games.

I have seen $100 million deals in which everyone was in agreement on the big things collapse over a concession that would have cost one side or the other a mere $3,000. Neither side felt they should be the ones to pay, and the deals got stuck in an endless round of attorney bargaining. Eventually, everyone walked away on a matter of principle. Only last year I watched from the sidelines as a tech startup received an offer of $5 million in venture capital. The startup's CEO was an attorney, and he could not resist negotiating every phrase and clause in the deal contract. I warned him to stop doing it because time is the enemy. Sure enough, a new general partner took over at the venture capital firm and said no new deals would be approved until he had reviewed every one in light of the firm's new direction. Sadly, that direction was away from the tech firm.

Unless your business involves negotiating the release of hostages, ignore much of the standard negotiating advice. It's not practical for the real business world. When it comes to negotiation, if you are a small entity, there are only two rules that I adhere to in order to successfully achieve effective contracts:

1. The one who mentions price first *loses*. No matter what number is thrown out at first, the purpose of negotiation, even the friendliest one, is to come to an

agreement, and the agreement will rarely be on that first number. Whatever price you throw out first, the final one will be different. It is smart, therefore, to always let the other side throw out a number first. It might pleasantly surprise you.

2. When you are a small company, don't get greedy. If you are offered a fair deal, take it. The aim is to survive long enough to get big enough to be able to push for a better deal.

Monitoring and Working with Vendors

The beginning of any relationship can have ups and downs and none more so than the relationship between your company and a new vendor. To ensure the fewest teething troubles as possible, it is essential to put a lot of effort into the initial education, training, and direction of the people who are responsible for your product or service.

Throughout the year, hold periodic refresher training using a webinar in which everyone can air their concerns, get questions answered, and exchange feedback. For customer-service personnel, provide binders with frequently asked questions and their scripted responses.

Since staff turnover at the vendor can also be an issue, ensure succession procedures are in place for new hires to receive immediate training on your product or service.

Then, let vendors do their job. Many entrepreneurs, including myself, are control freaks by nature. It takes courage to trust people and vendors to do what you are paying them to do without interference. You have to strike the right balance between being kept informed and being a royal pain in the backside for wanting constant updates.

My regular career had indoctrinated me with a belief that

everyone has to work at full pace and that there are not enough hours in the day to achieve everything necessary. With a virtual business, however, I have found the opposite to be true. I can have so much spare time on my hands I actually feel a bit guilty about it. As Lao Tse says, "The best leader is the one whose people say 'we did it all ourselves.'" The virtual business structure offers a distinct advantage in that regard.

Even when I go on vacation, the business operations just keep running. At first it was disconcerting that no one would notice my absence. But using the hub model, we have to empower vendors and keep out of the way, which can feel unnatural. Empowerment means allowing vendors to solve problems and make improvements freely.

Mitigate Risks with Backup Vendors

Replacing contractors who provide function expertise is not usually a problem, since there are lots of self-employed consultants in most markets. Replacing specialist vendors, however, can be a challenging issue, and sometimes vendors don't have well-run businesses. One time I relied heavily on a single manufacturer for product supplies. They had issues in a part of the company that was unrelated to my product, but the authorities closed down the whole plant. Finding another manufacturer at short notice and then getting them up to speed to provide product before we ran out of inventory was nothing short of a nightmare.

I learned my lesson, and from then on I ensured I always had a backup vendor in place. They were trained and ready, but kept in reserve. It cost a monthly management/retainer fee, but the cost was justified by the mitigation of risk. For any hard-to-replace function or task, have a backup vendor.

Further, because it took me so long to get a new manufacturer up to speed, I afterward also kept two years' worth of inventory volume on hand at the warehouse at all times. Sometimes we had to discard unused product that had expired, but that was better than running out of product if we had manufacturing issues. Customers are hard enough to find in the first place, and they will flee to the competition if you cannot supply them. Never run out of product.

Part of the Plan: Avoid Leasing Office Space

Most new entrepreneurs seem in a hurry to lease an office space for their new business, and their typical first purchase is a large sign of the company name to put over the entrance. That might be appropriate if your business is a retail store that will be visited by paying customers, but it is totally unnecessary for most startups using the hub model, in which the owner is the only employee. Even if your company is a quasi-hub, with one or two employees, I recommend having everyone work from home until the business becomes established and staff grows further.

Office facilities are not cheap. As well as the cost to rent, there will usually be a minimum rental period of perhaps six months or more. For most of that time, the office will be empty because the owner should be out and about trying to sell products or services. As well as the rental cost, here are the other costs to consider:

- Security
- Utilities
- Customizing signage and configuration to your company
- Receptionist
- Business property tax
- Heating, ventilating, air-conditioning

- Furniture and equipment
- Office supplies
- Janitorial services
- Maintenance and repairs

As with hiring too soon, leasing an office before you need one uses vital capital and impacts cash flow. Ask yourself honestly: Do you want an office as an ego boost, or is it genuinely essential? What will you do in your office that you can't do from home? If you will mainly sit at a computer and use the phone, why do you need a separate and expensive location to do that? In the early months and years of a company, cash flow is so critical to survival that it makes sense to consider alternative setups. Today's technology makes it easy to manage a business and be productive from home.

Whenever people hear the term *home-based office*, they often imagine small, part-time hobbyist endeavors or a desk shoved in a corner where employees telecommute from home a day or two a week. This is completely different from running a home office as an owner. In fact, the transition can be more difficult than it sounds, especially if you have only ever worked in an office and for large, structured companies that provide systems and administrative support, not to mention facility management. However, using the tips below, you can do it successfully and might even find it surprisingly fulfilling.

Working from Home: Tips and Strategies

Effective home offices and routines grow out of the same kind of insight that great companies do. They begin with people who can identify their own needs both as workers and as business owners. It is important not to assume that it will be an easy transition. You should prepare for it with the same attention to detail with which you create your business plan and manage cash flow.

You need to choose a suitable space in the home that will be your workplace. Then you must assess your business technology needs separately from the rest of the home. The early months of a new business are hectic, so the more efficiency and automation you can build into the setup before you start, the better it will be for you. You also must know and manage yourself in ways that help you develop a productive routine.

Create a Separate, Defined Office Space

An office space that is separate from the main home, and any family traffic, is preferred. This creates a physical boundary between work and home, which helps us mentally transition when we "go to work" in the morning and "return home" at night. It also helps family and houseguests to acknowledge and respect that work boundary. Sometimes, a home or apartment won't have an obvious, dedicated work space, so you must create one, perhaps by converting a basement, loft space, or guest bedroom. In a separate office space, background noises are less likely to disturb you, and if your family and children can't see you, the temptation to interrupt you goes away. Over time, your mind will adjust whenever you enter and leave your office space, which will help you stay disciplined when you're at work and help you relax in other parts of the home when you're not working.

Although it sounds obvious, a door that closes off your office space is essential. Even if outside noise is limited, shutting the door is necessary. It aids concentration, avoids distractions, and provides a more professional environment. Many times I have called a potential consultant on the phone and heard dogs barking or children playing in the background. This does not give a professional impression.

I also highly recommend making sure your office space has a window that gets natural daylight. I know people who work out of their basements without a view, and this is even more depressing than the neon-lit cubicles in most workplaces. There are lots of health benefits to having natural daylight pour in, but it also helps alleviate any sense of isolation from the world. On the other hand, if windows look onto views that are distracting (like city streets or oceans), fit the windows with blinds to let in light while filtering the view.

Use Dedicated Technology for Business

The office space and the business you run should have dedicated computers, printers, and communication devices. So many people have one device that is used for both business and pleasure. That means constant distractions during the workday and constant business intrusions during relaxation times. A balanced life requires discipline and separation. Your computer and communications devices must not be shared or accessible to others in your family, so no one else in the house can interrupt your productivity or accidentally answer your business calls. So much can be accomplished with a mobile device, but it is a mistake to think that the mobility of a device makes you productive simply because you can work from anywhere. As a customer, there is also nothing more annoying than when the businessperson you are speaking to gets interrupted by a personal call. One device must be dedicated only to work.

For instance, if someone uses the same smartphone for business, family, news, and gaming, then the temptation is too great to become distracted by reading a news alert or playing "just one game." Taking breaks is a good thing, but I suggest doing so by leaving the office and using an alternative device. Having separate devices may seem like an unnecessary expense at first, but it is critical to separate business and home and achieve a balanced life. As a rule of thumb, I have a smartphone, laptop, landline, tablet, and printer dedicated to my businesses. They are used for no other purpose. I never give my business email or telephone numbers to nonbusinesspeople or my domestic contact details to those I do business with. Most entrepreneurs I know use one device to handle business and pleasure, and their lives become chaotic and unproductive without them realizing why. Because most of your meetings will be video links, it is important to also invest in a professional microphone and camera that work well with your laptop or device. When you have those sessions, the background behind you should be one that does not distract anyone. A plain wall suffices.

For more detailed, nitty-gritty advice, see "Setting Up a Home Office" (pages 166–71), which walks you through organizing technology in your home office.

Create a Balanced, Disciplined Work Schedule

Working out of a home office can be a challenge to keeping a regular schedule. There are so many tempting distractions around: Family and friends might pop in for a chat, kids might need attention, the kitchen might beckon, laundry always needs to be done, or you might want to catch the last innings of an afternoon baseball game, check the stock market, play a video game, or get the news headlines.

At home, you are the time and office manager, and the secret to staying disciplined is to schedule absolutely everything, even your meditation time and coffee breaks, your trips to the gym and to the grocery store. Then, never deviate from the day's schedule.

On the other hand, it's also tempting to continue working

all the time. It's just as easy to let business intrude into one's personal life, so that dinner and time with family and friends is perpetually interrupted with work calls and emails. As they say, "All work and no play make Jack a dull boy." The key to successfully working from home and avoiding burnout is to practice both discipline and balance: Work when it's time to work, and play when it's time to play. At home, there are none of the typical distractions of an office — like impromptu meetings and coworkers stopping in to complain about the boss — and this allows us to be so much more productive. The downside is that our personal life and mental health can suffer if we don't take enough breaks and maintain firm boundaries when we are off the clock. However, the same schedule that keeps us on task can also be used to protect our free time. I recommend using online calendars. That way, you can block out one-hour breaks during the day, and you can send a calendar link to customers and clients, who can pick open schedule times for calls. That way no one will accidentally interrupt you when you are on a break or off work. Then, during a break, I suggest leaving your home office and interacting with the world. Work out, go for a walk, or even go grocery shopping.

This issue is so important that I consider it part of the "success mentality" you need to cultivate when pursuing a startup, and I address it further in chapter 9 (see "Schedule Discipline," pages 240–43).

Dress for Work

Other than opinion and anecdotes, there is no scientific evidence to suggest that how we dress at home affects our performance or productivity. Some people feel they are sharper if they dress well at home. Others think dressing casually increases creativity, and one of the great pleasures for me in being my own boss is that I never have to wear a tie. In fact, I no longer possess a single tie in my wardrobe. That said, dress as if you are going to work, as a way to mentally prepare for your day, and if you will be meeting clients or vendors, look appropriately professional.

For instance, there is clear scientific evidence that people make judgments about others based on what they see. People take everything in: skin color, gender, age, height, hairstyle, and clothes. Depending on what type of company you run, how you dress can have a significant bearing on how much business you get. This should be obvious, but I am frequently surprised by the sloppy appearance of businesspeople who visit my home to quote on a work project. Just because you are a plumber does not excuse you for dripping muck through my house or shaking my hand with dirty fingers. Just because it is hot does not excuse you for meeting business associates in crumpled shorts and a T-shirt. Similarly, when you are holding video meetings, you should appear as you would if meeting in person. I am always shaved. My hair, which I agree I am lucky still to have, is always neat, and I have a smart open-neck shirt. No one can see that I am also in shorts and with naked feet.

Keep Out of the Kitchen

A global study in 2015 by workplace provider Regus showed about a third of respondents reported worrying about gaining weight, since the proximity of a home fridge makes it so easy to snack throughout the day. It is not just the temptation of the snacks themselves, but the need to get away from the desk or computer for a bit. Working from home can feel isolating, and so it is all too easy to satisfy the need for a quick break by going to the kitchen, making coffee, and checking out the refrigerator.

Meandering through pantries to find a snack every time

you feel hungry can become a genuine distraction. Stay away from the kitchen. I find that having refreshments in my office stops me from falling for the temptation of the refrigerator. If I keep out of the kitchen, I cannot be tempted by food. I am a lover of Chinese teas, so I keep a pot on a warmer on my desk or patio table all the time. It stops me from sneaking into the kitchen and then getting distracted by the biscuit barrel.

Lock the Children in a Closet

No, not really. As a parent, you love your children. But work and childcare do not go together. If you have kids at home who are too young to manage themselves while you work, then you need to find an arrangement that saves you from this task.

I asked Sandy, the owner of a virtual-style marketing business, how she coped with running a company and having two young children at home. This is what she wrote:

> Two words: GET HELP! Just as in a traditional office situation, working parents will likely want to obtain some level of childcare for younger children. In my situation, there were early months when my newborn was very manageable while handling the tasks required of me. Additionally, the very flexible schedule I was given allowed me to work at nights (when my child was sleeping) or weekends (when my spouse could care for our child). However, as my child grew in mobility and increased in vocal ability/volume — usually timed strangely at the same time as any business/conference call — it became obvious I would need at least minimal daycare assistance. In my case, I had someone come to my home to provide daycare. Once there were two children and my schedule became less flexible, I increased the hours with my daycare provider.

The Challenges of Working from Home

Phil was the CEO of a tech company before he started his own business. After years of stressful commuting on congested freeways, he told me how much he was looking forward to the freedom of working from home.

Phil had spent all his working life in a fairly typical office environment. The company had a hierarchy of management, and no decisions were ever made without a meeting being held. His usual workday consisted of several rounds of meetings with department heads and phone conferences with his boards of directors and advisors. The schedule was kept for him by his assistant, who also brought him coffee at set times.

He usually skipped lunch in favor of a meeting, but every Friday he allowed the employees to dress casually for his weekly lunchtime staff meeting. His office door was always open, and he encouraged people to stop in for a chat. As commendable as that is, most employees are intimidated by the CEO title, so his most frequent visitors were the senior managers and the head of the human resources department.

Any habit, especially one formed over twenty years, is hard to change. The brain is hardwired to repeat certain behaviors, whether they are beneficial or harmful. When entrepreneurs transition from a traditionally structured company to a hub-model startup, they have to break many hardwired habits, and it is not easy. To suddenly go from a busy schedule of human interaction to the isolation of working from home can be as big an adjustment as transitioning to civilian life after military service or when graduating from college and jumping into the workplace.

I tried to warn Phil not to underestimate the difficulty. Adjusting to this transition can take months, and it requires great discipline to develop productive new habits while working from home. But like most people, Phil assumed it would be easy, and he largely ignored my advice. Sure enough, several months later, Phil confessed that he was finding the change very hard, and he was considering quitting his business to return to a regular job and office environment.

I visited him at his apartment, which was a luxury penthouse with panoramic views of the ocean. Floor-to-ceiling windows allowed sunlight to fill every space, and they looked down on a busy waterfront below. I asked him to show me his office space. With a sweep of his hand, he gestured around the apartment.

It transpired that Phil had made all the classic errors I had warned him to avoid. He admitted that he sometimes lay in bed later than he should, and on those days, he would simply stay in his pajamas, set up his laptop on the kitchen table, and start checking email first thing. This is a common temptation, but before he knew it, half the day was gone and he was still in his pajamas.

Often, he did not shower or shave until after midday. He had constant access to the refrigerator, and there were used dishes everywhere, which explained his extra pounds since he stopped commuting to an office.

He said loneliness was the hardest thing to adjust to. As a CEO, people sought him out, and his office was always busy. The constant pilgrimage to his office had been an ego boost. For the first few weeks, some of his ex-colleagues had phoned to see how he was doing with the new company venture, but eventually those calls fizzled out. Realizing his previous company was doing just fine without him added to his sense of loss. To alleviate the seclusion, he started calling *them*. It was like a retired coach who can't stay away from the training ground. Before long, people stopped picking up the phone.

Phil said that, although he liked the sense of freedom from the old routine, his new schedule was all over the place.

Sometimes he exercised in the mornings and caught up with work later at night. At other times, he put the TV on in the background and would check on newsfeeds while working. He admitted to being easily distracted by anything that could alleviate the loneliness.

Phil needed rehabilitation, and I started by getting him to promise that with everything he did and with every detail of his daily schedule, he would ask himself out loud: "Would this be appropriate behavior in a traditional office?" If something was inappropriate in his previous company, why would it be acceptable now? I asked him: "What would have happened when you were CEO if you sometimes lay in bed till noon or turned up to work in your slippers and pajamas? How productive would you have been if you worked on your laptop in the company cafeteria?"

For several weeks, we discussed the need for discipline, balance, and schedules, and I helped him strategize a new routine and home office space, using the advice in this chapter. Then, I did not meet up with Phil again for a couple of years, and by then I had forgotten the rehabilitation process we went through. I asked Phil how things went, and here is what he shared with me:

How difficult was the change?

"After twenty years of going to work outside my home, the transition to working at home was difficult, but manageable. It was stressful at first because I had to set up a home office, including updating my computer, learning to back up files, getting a copier/scanner/printer, upgrading my internet to faster service, setting up an accounting system, and so on. It sounds simple, but all this took time, and some of the tasks were things my personal assistant and staff used to do for me. I felt pretty dumb at the time, like a remedial student. It was humbling. The hardest single technical aspect of setting up the home business was the lack of IT support. In all my previous positions, I simply picked up the phone when I had any issue or question, and an IT expert was there to help. In my home office, I had to wade through my technical computer issues by myself. I tried calling a local IT support company a few times, but they were expensive. Consequently, I spent a lot of time learning technical computer stuff. But now I am the neighborhood expert."

How long did it take you to adjust?

"It took me about six months. I needed to get a routine going, and I had a couple of false starts with that. After you weaned me off daytime stock market TV, I started over. Initially, I thought I should keep it like a regular job. Start at 8 AM, work until noon, take an hour lunch, and then work until 5 PM. But that is way too intense at a home office. There are no meetings, nobody stopping by to chat. An eight-hour workday at home is more productive than spending sixteen hours at the old office. Burnout is a real risk. What ended up working best for me was to break up my day. Work for a few hours early in the morning; then go to the gym, come back, and work for a few more hours; then take another break, like a walk or errand; and then come back and finish up whatever work was needed that day. This schedule made the workday longer, but I found I was less tired and stressed at the end of it."

What did you enjoy most in your new workday?

"Flexibility. If I had a personal appointment that day, I could simply start earlier in the morning or work later in the evening. To take a break from the computer and phone, I could go shopping when things are less crowded. It is amazing how much more pleasant grocery shopping is in the middle of a weekday. In the winter, I could actually take a walk during daylight hours! A neighbor below me works nine to five, and her dog is shut in all day, so I started taking it for a short afternoon walk, which was good for everyone."

What did you miss the most about a regular office environment?

"Without a doubt, the thing I missed most was the day-to-day people contact and the relationships with other workers. I still miss the friends I made while working, and I needed to find an alternative way to connect with people. Let's face it, it is hard to have a good conversation with a dog! I joined an exercise group at the gym and got to know other work-at-home people. I talk to the neighbors and others more now because I have more time, and I am not always feeling so rushed. I also joined the local small-business owner's society. They are great ways for executives to meet and share best practices, but just as important is the social interaction."

Do you have any tips to help others make a successful transition?

"I think everyone needs to find out what works best for them, and don't be afraid to make changes if something is not working out. One of the best things about working at home is that your work hours are flexible. If you love to stay up to 2 AM, then go ahead, and use that time for work. The other thing is don't take on too much work or play. You need a balance, and it is really easy to stress yourself out by taking on more than you can handle. Most of all, though, I realize I almost blew it by not starting off right. Knowing what I know now, I would have spent time getting the office set up *before* I started my own thing. I lost so much traction and productivity early on, and only after six months was I back on track."

Setting Up a Home Office

My home office has changed from nothing grander than a piece of hardboard that lay across a spare bed to a custom-made casita. Regardless, the fundamentals of running a home office are the same. There are standard tools and tips that can make your home setup productive. There are certain pieces of equipment you must have, some software that helps with efficiency, and tricks you can utilize to save you time. Most new business owners that I meet have not paid attention to these matters before starting their company, and they end up getting unnecessarily distracted later.

In addition, I've found that a surprising number of people who start companies have limited technology skills. Like Phil, they never learned how to do certain tasks because those jobs were done by others in their company, and now they have to learn from scratch in order to set up their home office.

This section is for those people. Below, I offer tips and advice for people with little or no prior technology experience. Some readers may not need this information, and it is not meant to cover every available technology or update. However, hopefully this will cover the basics so you can be up and running with minimal fuss and aggravation.

Telephone Setup

With a virtual company, it is necessary to strike the right balance between keeping your company rapidly responsive to stakeholders and giving the stakeholders the perception of a larger organization than a one-person outfit. The complicated communication layers of a hierarchical company frustrate people, but they are equally leery of the small startup, which can be perceived as lacking structure and organization. The secret is to strike the right balance for perception, which is easily achieved with simple technology add-ons.

As annoying as some auto-attendee call systems can be, people still have a more favorable impression of a company when they encounter an attendant-answered phone service than if someone immediately reaches the business owner on their mobile phone while driving. Perception is important, and so long as the triage process is not onerous, you should set up a simple system that gives the impression of the customer reaching a formal place of work before being triaged to the appropriate decision maker.

Such a system has a dedicated phone number that answers a call with a brief message offering two or three options. Of course, regardless of which option the caller chooses, the call will forward to you or your voicemail, but the customer does not know that, and this creates the impression of a larger company.

These days there are lots of online companies that offer easy-to-use options for a home-based business call center. Just search "virtual auto-attendant." They are all relatively inexpensive because the competition is fierce. Some companies offer additional services such as a live call announcer and call-screening services that can give an even more polished response to callers. Whichever service you choose, it is a lot less costly than leasing an office and hiring a receptionist, which entrepreneurs do all too frequently.

Voice-over-the-internet systems have improved in quality in recent years. I use a service that provides an attendee response, a business line, a separate home line, unlimited calling anywhere in the world, and voicemail-to-email translation. I have used the same system for all my companies, and my monthly phone bill has never been over a hundred dollars.

Filing System and Data Storage

Today, many tech startups typically build their businesses with help from cloud computing services. These are services that provide instant access to computing power via the internet. Cloud computing simply means storing and accessing data and programs over the internet instead of on your computer's hard drive. The cloud is just a metaphor for the internet.

When you store data on or run programs from your computer hard drive, it is called *local* storage and computing. Everything you need is physically close to you, which means accessing your data is fast and easy for that one computer or for any others on the local network. A local network is usually sufficient for most startups and is certainly the cheapest option.

In my opinion the biggest issue for using cloud computing is the cost of its rental. While cloud computing is suited to many tasks, including getting your startup off the ground or running a modest website, it doesn't make sense for most startups while cash flow is still the essential factor to survival.

A recent article in *Wired* questioned the long-term costs of renting cloud services. For example, the ride-sharing startup Uber moved most of its tech off the Amazon cloud because its rental costs were ten times higher than achieving the same support with the purchase of physical servers. In the article, Kit Colbert, an engineer at VMware, said, "I don't know how much this is written about. Within IT departments, public clouds do tend to get more expensive over time, especially when you reach a certain scale."

Renting virtual servers from a company like Amazon seems more convenient for tech companies than buying a fleet of physical machines, and when you are at the startup phase, it may seem the sensible and flexible way to go, but for long-term plans, you should be wary of spiraling rental and user costs. For most service and physical-product companies, it may be best to use the storage capabilities of your computer's hard drive.

For the storage of administration matters, it is essential to keep copies of everything. All correspondence, financial matters, and operating procedures can be easily saved and organized with little effort these days. Technology today leaves no excuse for losing invoices, leads, or contact information.

Many companies often have someone who is responsible for keeping corporate files organized. Now that person is you. Also, because your network of vendors can be geographically dispersed, you need an easy way to share spreadsheets and documents. This is where cloud computing can help. One way is to set up an online file-sharing system and manage everyone's access. It is a bit like setting up a virtual data room that allows remote vendors and consultants to exchange information easily via uploads and downloads, and it is an excellent way to back up and organize all your files.

Countless choices of machines and systems exist today. However, this is not something you should put off until you find yourself overwhelmed by files. In the startup phase, you can get quickly engulfed by data and paper shuffling. Contracts go back and forth with revisions, and each revision needs to be tracked. Data arrives from several vendors at once and needs to be shared in real-time to allow other vendors access to the content. To handle all that oneself would be nothing short of a nightmare, but by using a file-sharing portal, the system does the work for you.

The same file-sharing system can be used to store all your cash-flow, financial, and expense reports, along with tax papers, corporate registration paperwork, and so on. You simply organize the file system like a series of rooms in a building, and then enjoy the experience of an uncluttered desk.

Computers and Devices

If you don't already have a computer and a smartphone, or another internet-capable communications device, you would be crazy to start a business without them. However, I did meet a small-business owner recently who used only a paper diary to run her business, and she was more organized than most entrepreneurs I meet. Budget may determine what you can use, and if your finances are tight, make sure your main device is portable.

In this information age, you need to be able to write presentations while commuting and to access email while sitting in waiting rooms or browsing the grocery aisles. You need all the basic business software, which includes email, spreadsheets, and presentation design programs.

Right now, I use a desktop in the home office, a light laptop outdoors, and a tablet when I travel. They communicate with one another, so that I am able to access the updated files on whichever device I use. I have no recommendations for one system or device over another. My main concern for the startup entrepreneur is that devices and their screens get smaller and smaller. That is great for traveling, but it is a detriment to giving presentations to prospective customers or potential investors. Think of balancing budget, technological capability, and the practicality of getting your pitch across. Your laptop may be your storage device, but it may also have to double as your presentation vehicle.

This is my main concern with computers and devices: Be ready at all times to present your business to prospective clients, customers, vendors, and investors. When opportunities show themselves, it is not always in a controlled environment. All the best deals I have made have been chance encounters, such as in an airport lounge, waiting in line for coffee, or a brief conversation in a hallway. For that reason, you should have a copy of your pitch in every format (hard copy, brochure, flash drive, recorded on a mobile device) and with you at all times, then select the one most suitable to the occasion.

There is nothing worse than having a chance meeting with a great prospect and then fumbling through your briefcase or handbag for a crumpled brochure. You need to have a slick way of responding to the prospect's interest. If you can professionally slip out a device from a pocket, and with a practiced, polished maneuver, immediately bring up a slideshow or diagram, all the better.

Printers and Scanners

You should get the best-quality printer you can afford. We all judge the materials that come in the mail or get thrust into our hands. When materials look homemade, they become useless as marketing tools, so this is one area where you should avoid the cheap, all-in-one solution.

If you worked in a regular office, you probably never gave much thought to the cost of printing supplies or ink, or you never hesitated to make lots of printed copies of reports. I have worked with people who refused to review electronic files and insisted on hard copies of everything. Printers are cheap, but printer supplies are not. Only print something if it is absolutely essential for the business.

Desktop Post Office

Several online options exist for adding post office and courier shipping capabilities from home. The ones I have used for the last decade have no service or membership fees at all, and they have served me perfectly well. I am able to order supplies for free, weigh packages, print labels and postage, and arrange for pickup all with a few mouse clicks. Technology means there is no reason to have to drive to a shipping depot or post office anymore. Simply search online and choose from the many options.

PART III

THRIVING

My mission in life is not merely to survive, but to thrive;
and to do so with some passion, some compassion,
some humor, and some style.

— Maya Angelou

We all judge success in different ways. For some it is about getting rich. For others it is about self-actualization. Some people crave to be recognized or rewarded. Others, like myself, might want to prove the doubters wrong.

For a business, however, there is really only one parameter for success: being profitable. Even a nonprofit has to make enough money to cover its costs. Making a positive difference and fixing problems are necessary ingredients for coming up with a winning idea, but all by themselves, they won't make a successful business. Unless a company is eventually profitable, it will cease to exist, and then whatever good the entrepreneur hoped to achieve will be lost as well. Profit isn't necessarily the first thing someone should think about when contemplating a business, but it shouldn't be the last, either.

Then again, profit can be defined in various ways. In the simplest terms, profit is the amount of money left over after all revenue has been received and all costs paid. For startups, being profitable in this way can take years, which is why it's important to have sufficient capital and to manage cash flow. However, some businesses, like my current one, focus mainly on incubating inventions, with the goal of being eventually acquired by a larger company, which also can take years. Profit, therefore, could be defined as a financial return or reward that eventually exceeds the risk and investment made.

Part 3 focuses on how to achieve that return on investment by turning a well-conceived startup into a thriving business. That depends on several things. First, ensuring that the startup's winning idea has been shaped into a winning product or service, and then promoting it through a great marketing campaign. Beyond making sales, however, marketing and the company's image need to cultivate a trustworthy relationship with customers — so that people feel good about doing business with you and eagerly return. Finally, all of this depends on developing the right mentality for success. That mentality is a collection of attitudes that balance adaptability with discipline, leadership with fun. When all these ingredients come together, it's a recipe that leads to multimillion-dollar successes.

CHAPTER SEVEN

Great Marketing and the Secret of Sales

*Sales are contingent upon the attitude of the salesman —
not the attitude of the prospect.*

— W. Clement Stone

In order for a startup to become a successful business, the winning idea that inspired the entrepreneur needs to be shaped into a winning product or service. Ideally, that should not be too difficult, since any winning idea should already embody all the attributes of a winning product, which is the foundation of success. The real challenge is marketing and selling in effective ways in our current era of rapid customer feedback. There is no shortcut here. Great marketing and sales use simple, enduring concepts that do not change, no matter how much technology changes. Just target the right customers with the right message the right number of times, make it easy to recommend, and close the sale.

What Makes a Winning
Product or Service

What makes a great product or service is always a hot debate among commercial experts. To me, it includes four essential attributes, two of which should be part of any winning idea: It has a defined purpose, and it makes someone's life better. However, it should also be simple to use, and customers should feel that it exceeds their expectations. In fact, you should consider all four attributes when first conceiving of your winning idea (see chapter 1), and they should be included and described in your business plan (see chapter 3). Then, your marketing and sales will be built around promoting these four qualities.

1. It Has a Clearly Defined, Singular Purpose

If something makes you so mad you want to create a product to fix it, you can almost guarantee that you are focused on a singular purpose. That is essential. Too many products try to be all things to all people. A product that satisfies a singular purpose is easy to understand, and its value is easy to calculate. As I discuss below, simplicity is the most important marketing tool when it comes to helping consumers make a purchase decision. Simplicity starts with the product.

When Google was first introduced in 1998, many questioned why it would even bother with a search engine. AltaVista had already come to define the genre, and for the most part, people thought the internet search problem was essentially solved. However, through its singular focus using a search box offered on an otherwise blank page, Google quickly became the leader. It was just simple for people to use.

Identifying a singular issue and providing one clear solution makes a great product. With services, doing one thing better than anyone else is the starting point. Being as good as or different in some minor way is not enough. Be the best at one clearly defined thing.

I have used several housecleaning companies in the last few years. There are lots of companies to choose from, and it is hard to differentiate them. The first one advertised their use of only eco- and pet-friendly products, and that appealed to me. Staff turnover at the company, however, was an issue for them because cleaning houses is harder work than most employees anticipate. Each time a three-person team arrived at my house, all the faces were new, which required me to explain what they had to do all over again, and I eventually got fed up.

I went with another company that had rave internet reviews, but it was quickly obvious that their teams cut corners, so I ditched them. A third company advertised the lowest rates, but when three men showed up with about half a dozen teeth between them, I did not even let them in the house.

Finally, I found a cleaning service that fixed this staffing problem in a remarkably simple way. They are a family. Mother, father, sons, daughters, and cousins all work for the one company. They understand that I want my house to be taken care of as carefully as their house, and also that I don't want strangers turning up at the front door all the time. The only problem? I had to join a waiting list because they could only take on a certain number of clients. When finally there was a space, I hired them.

Their business has created a winning product. I'm comforted when familiar faces turn up every month, which has established trust, and it makes them easy to use, since I don't have to repeat instructions. Their business has a clearly defined, singular purpose — to clean homes like a family cleans their own home — and yet they also exceed expectations, since the father doubles as a handyman when things need fixing. They have changed my life for the better.

2. It Changes People's Lives for the Better

If your product does not improve people's lives, it is not a winning idea, and no amount of marketing will make a difference. People will only recommend your product to others when they are emotionally excited. To do that, the product has to improve their quality of life in some way. All this might seem like common sense, but we live in a world with so many choices that just trying to decide can be a source of frustration.

I had a friend who tried to launch her own line of dog shampoos. No matter how many times I asked her to explain what difference the product made in people's lives, she answered that the pretty pink label was more eye-catching. The same generic manufacturer that supplied all the other dog-shampoo companies made hers. So despite her distinctive labeling and attempts at branding, her business never took off. Savvy branding is not enough. People can easily research beyond the label and beyond the choices on the shelves to make informed decisions. Your product or service must make a difference in the purchaser's life.

3. It's Simple to Use, Simple to Upgrade, Simple to Fix

A few years back I had a customized home theater installed. The system was relatively simple to use, but a nightmare to fix. Frequent automatic software and firmware updates paralyzed it, and I had no choice but to call a technician to fix it. This happened every few months, and the technician spent hours wandering around my home trying to work out the cause of the problem.

Most of the equipment was by one manufacturer, and my experience meant I don't recommend that brand to others who are considering installing systems.

One time after an upgrade, the system no longer communicated with my controllers. The manufacturer told me that I would have to buy new controllers. Instead, I went online and downloaded an app that allowed me to use my smartphone as a controller. Now I am a big fan of the app maker who solved my issue, providing a product that is simple to use, simple to upgrade, and simple to fix. Now I recommend that app to everyone who cares to listen.

4. It Exceeds Expectations

It almost goes without saying that if we are not satisfied with a product, we rarely purchase it again. If I read a book by an author who is new to me, and it exceeds my expectations, I always look to see what else the author has written. The opposite happens when a book disappoints. Product experience, however, is only part of the equation for how we measure expectation. If I go to a restaurant and eat great food, but the waiter is surly, my overall expectation for dining out has not been met. I go to a restaurant for the total experience of the atmosphere, service, and quality of food.

This is true for any business. Customers pay attention to the total experience, which includes customer service, packaging, instructions, return policy, ease of payment, and so on. This is one reason why a winning idea is sometimes not enough to make for a winning business. Not only must the product itself be excellent, but someone's entire interaction with the product and the business must be satisfying. Further, customer expectations are easily influenced and set through social media and online reviews. This is a double-edged sword. You need a winning product or service that exceeds expectations to generate great reviews, but negative reviews or a lackluster marketing presence can hurt expectations even when a product is great.

New Technology Doesn't Change Marketing Techniques

The first paid advertisement published in a newspaper was in 1836, and the first recorded mass marketing of unsolicited spam was in 1864 using the telegraph. Since then, every new technology has attracted marketers like bears to honey. Telemarketing, relationship marketing, guerrilla marketing, and viral marketing have all been touted as the keys to success at one time or another. One could argue that the history of marketing is nothing greater than a history of communication fads. Every few years a new tool kit appears that promises to revolutionize business and marketing.

Those revolutions are short-lived. When a new communication medium appears, there is a small window of opportunity in which a marketer can reach a wide audience simply because the medium is new. Then, saturation occurs quickly, return on investment diminishes, and the old marketing rules reassert themselves. Unless an entrepreneur is the first to identify the power of the new medium and has the cash to exploit it, they will find it hard to get noticed among all the clamor and noise of the herd that is also rushing to it.

Unfortunately, I am old enough to recall when fax machines were such a novelty in the office that, the moment the machine started whirring, people ran from all corners as if their desks had caught fire to read whatever spewed out. Although the fax had been around for decades, it was only after Sony flooded the market with cheaper and lighter units in the 1980s that every small business adopted it as a cutting-edge communication tool.

When our office bought its first machine, people crowded around it as first one gray line appeared and then another. Like some office game of charades, everyone tried to guess what the final picture or message would be.

Very quickly, marketers saw an opportunity and started broadcasting promotions via fax. It was not much longer before people became fed up with running to the fax machine only to be offered another discounted cruise to Mexico.

When they were novel, fax campaigns offered marketers a good return on investment. Because the machine printed a piece of paper and someone had to physically remove that paper and either distribute or trash it, the "open" rate (which refers to people actually reading the message) was high. Once saturation happened, small-business marketers realized fax campaigns had little or no return on their investment. They stopped doing it, and most probably vowed never to follow the herd mentality again. That is, until the next fad came along, and the next one, from CD mailings, email blasts, online video, and social media tactics to smartphone apps, and so on, all the way up to today.

In fact, some marketers might argue that the ROI on fax campaigns today is higher again because it would stand out from the crowd of email and social media. Certainly some cultures like Japan still rely heavily on fax machines and fax communication, and some highly regulated industries have procedures that legally require fax copies. The herd, however, has moved on.

This obsession with technology is not new, and it infects all aspects of business. The most dramatic recent example is the dot-com bubble, which occurred between 1997 and 2000. High-tech startups attempting to profit from the internet and the wave of new communications technologies seemed poised to reinvent business, and almost everyone with access to a computer started trading tech stocks, hoping to get rich quick.

NASDAQ soared to previously unimagined heights due to this rampant speculation. Companies with dubious business plans, and questionable management experience, became famous overnight, all on the promise of eventually creating products and services using these new technologies that would somehow, in some way, benefit someone at some point.

Warren Buffett, who is today widely considered the most successful investor of the twentieth century, became a target of media and public criticism for ignoring the high-tech craze and even claiming he didn't understand it. Day traders called him a dinosaur for refusing to invest in internet companies. The dot-com revolution was a kind of changing of the guard, people said. The Dow Jones Industrial Average was dead, and NASDAQ, the new technology exchange, would take over.

Calmly responding to the criticism, Buffett stated simply that no matter how much he liked the technologies, he had trouble understanding which of the dot-com companies had the basic fundamentals required to succeed as a business. Most, he predicted, would never make it because their business plans were fundamentally flawed, and that is indeed what happened. Herd speculation reached a saturation point, the market collapsed, and by 2008, most of the dot-com companies had disappeared. The few spectacular survivors that are now household names and financial successes are also those that adhered to the fundamentals of business, which did not and have not changed.

The more things change, the more they stay the same. And what's true for business is true for marketing and sales. Warren Buffett didn't refuse to invest in tech companies just because they were tech companies; he refused to invest in uncertain startups and unproven businesses.

This is the same approach you should take when strategizing an effective marketing plan. Don't pursue a fad just because everyone is doing it. Today, I get inundated with offers from companies to build my social media campaign. At least twenty social media platforms, such as Myspace, Ping, and Yahoo Buzz, have been touted as the marketer's ideal tool kit, but they failed within a few years. It's easy to waste money and time marketing ineffectively on unproven platforms, and like Warren Buffett, I find it impossible to predict which social media company will survive long enough to get me a return on a campaign. That said, if social media is the best way to connect the right product to the right customer in the right way, then it should of course be part of the mix. The secret is to pick a company that is both inexpensive and knowledgeable about all the latest fads.

Communication technologies come and go, and the small-business entrepreneur usually cannot compete with large companies that try to take advantage of the short window of opportunity a new fad offers. Instead, keep to the basics, which never change: If you create a winning product, follow a winning marketing campaign, and create a trustworthy relationship with customers, you will be a successful business.

The Recipe for Great Marketing

Great marketing is not about joining all the noise, but standing out from it. To do that we have to get the right message to the right people the right number of times, and then make it easy and cool for them to pass the message to others.

The Right Message

In marketing lingo, products have "benefits" and "features." A *feature* is a fact about a product or service, while a *benefit* is what need or problem the feature solves for the customer. The right message highlights benefits, or how the product will make someone's life better.

A classic example used to explain the difference between

features and benefits is to consider an advertisement for a self-setting alarm clock. The facts that it is self-setting and also an alarm clock are features, which on their own don't name the solution they offer. Features may be interesting, but they are usually not compelling enough to make us do something... like buy the product. To market a self-setting alarm clock, consider what benefit the features provide for the customer. How do they improve someone's life? What need do they satisfy? One possibility is *convenience*. The jet-lagged traveling businessperson can plug it in and never miss a meeting again.

Even the biggest and most famous companies that spend billions on TV commercials make the basic marketing error of speaking about features rather than benefits. Car commercials can be the worst offenders, as they reel off a list of features about speed or technical capabilities without helping you grasp the benefits of them. For a car, the right message wouldn't talk about features like the engine's horsepower or the variety of safety features. Instead, the right message would focus on the main benefits of this particular car — say, that driving it could save your life during a car crash. The right message highlights a potentially life-changing benefit to the consumer. Another feature might be that the car is electric and doesn't use gas. Well, so what? The benefit always answers that question. In this case, the benefit might be feeling good that, while driving this car, you are minimizing your impact on the environment.

The Right Person

Although the convenience of the self-setting alarm clock is a benefit for travelers, it may not be relevant to all the customers you're targeting. In this case, that might be all people who use alarm clocks. So what about someone who is at home, like parents? Put yourself in the shoes of each particular, potential customer and ask, "What benefit really matters to them?" Perhaps the self-setting feature means a mom doesn't have to struggle with the instruction manual, her reading glasses, and then look like a complete fool in front of her twelve-year-old daughter, who could set it up without even taking her eyes off the TV.

That would be the true benefit to the mother: "No instructions necessary. Open the box and plug it in." To the daughter, the true benefit might be that she can give it as a gift to her mother knowing that, since it's so easy to use, she won't get all stressed out. The benefit to the daughter is a delighted mother.

The smart marketer has a couple of choices. When marketing to just travelers, you would highlight convenience; when targeting to just parents, marketing would highlight ease of use. In situations where both customer segments are targeted, the right message would combine these benefits: "Never fumble with a dial or miss an appointment again, wherever you are. The *simply-smart* alarm clock. Open the box. Plug it in. The smart alarm does the rest. It sets and resets itself. It is one smart alarm clock."

The secret to matching the right message with the right person is to constantly ask, "What are the benefits of each feature, and who needs those benefits?" One way to brainstorm this is to write out a list of features for your product or service. After each one, add the words, "Which means that," and then complete the sentence as if looking through the customer's eyes. Keep adding "which means that" until you have as many benefits as you can think of. For example: "Feature: self-setting alarm clock. Which means that…all you have to do is plug it in; which means that it sets the time for you; which means that there is no manual to read; which means that there are no fiddly knobs and dials; which means that you don't need to find your reading glasses or get stressed."

These are things you should think through and strategize

as you create your business plan (see chapter 3). In the plan, describe the demographics and profile of your target potential customers and name the benefits your product provides those customers. Online marketing tools, such as those provided by Google, Facebook, and others, provide plenty of analytical products that can segment their site visitors so you can more accurately target a defined demographic with the right message. That helps to make your marketing budget more impactful, with a higher profitability for each dollar spent on advertising.

The Right Number of Times

In order to plan efficient TV media buys, 1960s advertising expert Herbert Krugman researched how many times consumers needed to see a commercial for the same product or brand before taking an action. His conclusion is studied in many marketing classes as the "theory of effective frequency for advertising."

Repetition is the basis of any learning process, and it's no different for consumers learning about a product. Krugman initially concluded that the magic number was three. In other words, after seeing or hearing about a product or brand three times, consumers would take an action. Here is a summary of his findings:

- The first time someone is exposed to your message, you attract their attention, but nothing is really taken in. Thus, they ask, *"What is it?"*
- The second time, the consumer begins to engage with the relevance of the message and asks, *"So what?"*
- And the third exposure is when the viewer decides whether to buy the product or to forget it.

Later research has suggested the number is more than three. Nielsen media guru Erwin Ephron's work led him to conclude it was five times. More recently, a Nielsen study claims ten social media touches are needed to effect a behavior change, but that may also just reflect the fact that social media is difficult to market in successfully, especially if you're doing it yourself rather than using an expert vendor. The point is that you've got to get your product in front of your customers multiple times in order for them to take the action you want.

The great thing about digital marketing is that there are many cost-effective ways to achieve your multiple marketing touches: email, social media, display advertising, websites, microsites, sponsorships, content marketing, and so on. But there's also a limit to this. How much pushing messages at potential customers is too much? A 2012 *Harvard Business Review* article suggested:

Marketers see today's consumers as web-savvy, mobile-enabled data sifters who pounce on whichever brand or store offers the best deal. Brand loyalty, the thinking goes, is vanishing. In response, companies have ramped up their messaging, expecting that the more interaction and information they provide, the better the chances of holding on to these increasingly distracted and disloyal customers. But for many consumers, the rising volume of marketing messages isn't empowering — it's overwhelming. Rather than pulling customers into the fold, marketers are pushing them away with relentless and ill-conceived efforts to engage.

It is a balancing act, and for the startup, the most cost-effective approach is to choose the channels that get the best responses. Which are they? Go ask your customers when you create your business plan.

Testing the effectiveness of any one medium, however, is tricky. For instance, say that two customers purchase after five impressions, but for one customer the fifth impression was email, and for the other it was an advertisement in a journal. The only way to know which media are effective is to ask your customer. That is why so many "How did you hear about us?" surveys pop up after we hit the purchase button. For marketing, this is essential data. The more information you have on that before you spend on advertising, the better. That is why it is so important to get away from your desk and talk to customers during the business-plan process. Just ask the customer what channels they pay attention to and hopefully a pattern will emerge.

Easy to Recommend

Think of products like Dropbox, Hotmail, or Snapchat and how quickly those products went viral with very little marketing effort. They were great products, each with a simple, singular purpose, and easily recommended via a strong message of benefit for the user. People enjoyed their experience, and the companies made it easy and exciting for them to share their enthusiasm with friends and family.

The same *Harvard Business Review* article focused on what makes consumers "sticky": "That is, likely to follow through on an intended purchase, buy the product repeatedly, and recommend it to others.... The single biggest driver of stickiness, by far, was 'decision simplicity' — the ease with which consumers can gather trustworthy information about a product and confidently and efficiently weigh their purchase options. What consumers want from marketers is, simply, simplicity."

The article also found that most marketers misjudge what

consumers want from them online. In particular, marketers often believe that consumers interact with them on social media to join a community and feel connected to the brand. But consumers have little interest in having a relationship beyond the transactional. In the study, 61 percent of consumers said they interacted on social media for discounts, reviews, and rankings, while 73 percent of marketers assumed that interaction was because customers want to learn more about a product. They have it wrong.

The article's survey found that brands lead consumers down unnecessarily confusing purchase paths with too many options. It concluded: "Often what a consumer needs is not a flashy interactive experience on a branded microsite but a detailed exchange with users about the pros and cons of the product and how it would fit into the consumer's life."

Too much choice can be paralyzing. One of the most common consumer responses to too much choice is to forgo a purchase altogether. In a classic experiment, Sheena Iyengar, then a doctoral student and now a professor at Columbia Business School, set out pots of jam on supermarket tables in groups of either six or twenty-four. About 30 percent of those who were given six choices bought some jam; only 3 percent of those confronted with twenty-four choices did. Too much choice or too much information can be paralyzing.

The survey concluded that marketers who focus on simplifying consumers' decision-making will rise above the din, and their customers will stick by them and recommend them as a result.

Getting Medicine to Patients: Marketing in Action

As an example of what this great marketing recipe looks like in action, let's consider my first company and the second product it produced, which was a treatment for a very rare disease. I can't claim that I did everything right, but overall I got the right message to the right people the right number of times and made it easy to recommend.

This started with the business-plan process. Since this treatment cured a rare disease, I knew I had a winning product with a life-changing benefit. To create a successful business, however, I had to answer a key question: Who was the target customer? Was it the patient with the disease or the physician who would treat it? There are strict regulations about marketing to both audiences, and to market directly to patients back then was not allowed at all. Even today, the vast majority of physicians in the world have never heard of this disease, and they would be unlikely ever to encounter it.

Mass marketing was a nonstarter due to the high cost of trying to get the right message the right number of times to every physician in the hopes that the right ones would see it. The "great marketing" challenges I faced were many: how to find those patients who would use the product, how to get them to a doctor who knew about the disease and would prescribe the product, how to find and educate those doctors, and how to get their health-care system to permit and then pay for the product. My marketing budget was less than $50,000.

As part of the business-plan process, I visited and interviewed a variety of specialist physicians about their opinions on the disease and our product. After months of conversations, it became clearer that sub-specialist groups of pediatric endocrinologists and pediatric gastroenterologists had the most interest in finding and treating these patients. From a database of millions of physicians, my early adopter list shrank to a manageable 1,200. Now I had a niche market that a smaller budget could reach.

From the research I also learned that this sub-specialist

group loved nothing better than standing on a podium to teach other less-specialized pediatricians how to treat better. I'm sure this was an ego boost, but mostly these doctors really cared about directing appropriate diagnosis and treatment.

It would have been pointless to hire a sales force or to use standard push marketing tactics to try to influence such opinion leaders. Push marketing is a strategy whereby a company advertises at the target audience to convince them to purchase a product or buy into an idea. What these subsets of pediatricians wanted was cold, hard data of efficacy and a way to teach that data and the benefits of the medicine to other pediatricians to help them find, diagnose, and treat the right patients. That had more of a community feel to it, so I chose to use pull marketing, which is a strategy for gathering groups and empowering advocates to build brand loyalty. A company pulls people in to form a bond and a group mentality.

The tactic I chose initially was to invite groups of eight to ten "key opinion leaders" in all the major cities in America and Canada to an educational meeting. That allowed me to get the right message to the right people. The inventor of the product gave a presentation, which was followed by discussion.

Once they understood the data and the disease, these pediatricians were able to identify problem patients they had been unable to help for years and who could be suffering from this disease. We agreed on a plan of action to help them find, diagnose, and treat these patients.

I followed up with each physician by mail and email, and by providing samples of the product to their practices. A few patients were diagnosed, and I made the treatment decision simple by shipping free finished product to the doctor's office so that the doctor could immediately experience the benefit through the patient's response to the medicine.

The results were immediate, and the treating physicians

were so delighted, they couldn't wait to tell others. I made it easy for them to recommend the product by providing speaker packages they could use at their regional specialty educational meetings. The speaker packages were approved by their national association, which added the same credibility as one would get today from trustworthy online reviews.

I also committed to everyone that we would ship free product to any newly diagnosed patient's physician for as long as it took us to work out payment with their health-care system and providers. When about thirty patients had been identified, diagnosed, and treated, with startling life-changing results, I encouraged these patients and their families to form a private online support group. That way they could help one another, but they would also find ways to echo their message online. Within a year, this group had attracted a hundred patients who had previously thought they were alone with their issues, and eventually over three hundred patients worldwide were diagnosed and treated.

Eventually, about 25 percent of patients got their product for free from my company for life. That sounds like a lot of lost revenue, and I had a few internal battles with investors over it, but what giving it to patients for free did was create brand and company loyalty. Physician groups and patient-advocacy groups were so delighted that brand loyalty, or stickiness, was 100 percent. Without any encouragement from me, they went out on social media and found new patients to bring into the fold.

We were so original and famous for doing this that my little company even got mentioned in what's called "Prime Minister's Question Time" in the UK Parliament. Imagine if I had refused to give away free product and even one patient remained sick? Stickiness would have plummeted.

I didn't do it for that reason. I did it because it was the

right thing to do, and it's what other pharmaceutical companies could and should do, and since then, many others have followed suit. As my mother used to say, *Doing the right thing is never the wrong thing to do.*

From a "great marketing" perspective, the pull tactics worked because the product was curative with very few side effects. Soon physicians started to use it as a sort of "suck it and see" diagnostic test, meaning that if a suspected patient responded well to taking the medicine, it was likely they had the disease. Then they were sent for a confirmatory diagnosis.

Although I had plenty of missteps along the way, this campaign was a success because it held to the fundamentals of a great product and great marketing.

The Secret of Sales

There is a secret to selling. Of course, this is a book about secrets, so here is another. The moment you try to sell something to someone is the moment you stop selling, and the moment you stop trying to sell something to someone is the moment you start selling.

Contrary to what most experts teach, selling is simply the process of meeting another human being and then listening to what they have to say. It really is that simple. Imagine walking into a room, meeting a family member, and sensing intuitively that something is troubling that person. Your senses perceive their glum expression and that something is "off" about their energy.

Because you care about their welfare, you ask them if everything is okay. Typically, they will brush off your concern. So what do you do? Push and pry? No, you respect their denial and stay quiet, knowing that eventually the simple act of silence will cause them to spill the beans.

In my opinion, a good sales process is exactly like that. Potential customers have needs. They have problems that need fixing. Your job is to meet them to find out what those needs are. If you can fix those needs, you will both be happy. If you can't, you will try to find someone else who can help that person, even if that someone else is your biggest competitor.

As the owner of a startup, the first thing you must accept is that, regardless of how you feel about sales, the biggest mistake you can make is to hire someone to do this function for you. One day you may need to hire a sales force, but if you have not performed the role yourself for at least a year, you will never be able to direct the sales force effectively because you will be out of touch with what your customers think and need. Another secret of sales is that it provides the best education you can get into your business. So while preparing your business plan and even after your business has started, be prepared to leave your office and go meet some customers...and listen to them.

Embrace Your Inner Salesperson

The process of selling intimidates a lot of startup entrepreneurs. Cultural and societal attitudes often portray the sales process as being aggressive or pushy. Most people like to be loved and approved of, and they take rejection personally. Many of us have also experienced the hard sell of a telemarketer, salesperson, or street-corner vendor and wrongly assume that is what selling is all about.

A Gallup poll on the honesty of business professionals found that insurance salespeople and car salespeople ranked worst. Perhaps that's not surprising. The poll also showed that more than 85 percent of customers have a negative view of *all* salespeople.

I know I did. My father was the stereotypical pushy salesman. Cigarette dangling from his lips, he was never short of
false confidence and charm when he manned his market stall
or the store we lived over. He could persuade people of just
about anything. "He could sell sand in a desert" was how others described him. It was obvious that he cared little about the
customer and everything about getting their money. That is
what I thought the sales process was all about: making a sale at
the expense of the "dumb" customer, which was always a one-
time thing, like winning a battle.

A decade later, I therefore felt a great deal of trepidation
when I decided to quit my secure job at a hospital to start a new
career as a sales representative for a pharmaceutical company.
My decision was purely for financial reasons. The entry-level
trainee position paid twice as much as my previous salary. I recall being shy and intimidated when I arrived at the company
headquarters for a five-week training course.

To my complete surprise, the other trainees were more like
me than my father. They were not pushy or extroverted. They
seemed honest and considerate of the customer. To my greater
surprise, the trainers were just as down to earth.

The content of the course taught us the rudiments of successful sales. Whereas I expected to be taught what to say and
how to say it, they taught me instead to listen to what the customer had to say. When I thought I needed to push the benefits
of the product, they trained me to know its limitations and to
assist the customer only with what they needed.

Not only was I relieved, but I thrived at the sales process. I
found I was a good listener, and it felt natural to want to help
a customer solve a problem. I had worked in a cancer hospital,
and all my work was about caring for people. I found sales was
more like that than about getting something for myself, which
was how my father approached sales. I took to selling like a

duck takes to water, and I never looked back. In all my own companies, my mantra has been, "The customer comes first, the rest is just detail." That is what that first course taught me, and I have never wavered.

Before I started as a sales trainee, I would never have imagined that one day I would consider myself something of an expert in the sales process, or that I would experience such fun and fulfillment in that role. I did, however, because I realized straightaway that the best salespeople are those who listen more than they speak. In sales, the introverts actually rule over the extroverts. Lucky for me.

Susan Cain, the author of *Quiet: The Power of Introverts in a World That Can't Stop Talking*, is an introvert. Intuitively, Cain felt that as an introvert she had value. Introversion isn't about being antisocial or shy; it's about how someone responds to external stimulation. I have often been called Mr. Even and also emotionally mature. Neither is true, but that's the impression I give because I don't show a lot of external signs of emotion when something goes well or not so well. When I sold my first company and banked my first financial success, I celebrated by spending the whole day in my PJs reading a new historical-fiction novel. It seemed perfectly normal to me. Others might have gone on a pub crawl or cracked open the champagne, and that is fine for them. While extroverts crave social interaction, introverts are much more alive while they're alone.

As Cain points out, we live in a culture that increasingly values groupthink. We believe that creativity comes from a very oddly gregarious place. Introverts are routinely passed over for leadership roles. That's a real problem because research has shown that, as leaders, introverts are more careful, much less likely to take outsize risks, and more likely to let creative and proactive team members run with their own ideas, rather than run over them or squash them — something that should be an ideal trait in the modern office, a startup, or a sales team.

I have never forgotten, however, my initial fear of sales because I thought it meant I had to act like an extrovert, and I meet many entrepreneurs who have difficulty with this aspect of running a business. An army of self-styled experts makes the process of sales overly complicated, which adds to the fear. They add jargon like "opening benefit statement," "active listening," and "trial closing," and it all starts to feel like you are learning to sell used cars with corny, stomach-churning questions, such as, "What would it take for me to get you into this vehicle?"

Take my advice. Ignore all that. I can easily take that fear away. I can tell you that everyone can succeed at selling with just a simple understanding of what the process entails. I did.

Effective Sales in Three Easy Steps

Selling can be one of the most rewarding tasks you'll undertake as a business owner if you follow these three simple steps: introduce yourself, have a conversation, and close the sale.

1. Introduce Yourself

As you approach a potential customer, imagine the person is your favorite relative. Don't run up and jump into their arms or plant a kiss on the cheek. Stand straight. Look the person between the eyes at the point where the nose meets the brow. This is clinically proven to make you both comfortable and secure. Direct eye contact, especially in certain cultures, can be off-putting for either party. Offer a firm but brisk handshake. Smile and be nice.

Practice a standard introduction in front of a mirror or on

an iPhone recording at least a hundred times. Keep it simple: "Hello, [name of person], I am Trevor, the owner of [name of business], and I am happy to answer any questions you have about how I can help your company grow faster."

The purpose of practicing this introduction is simply to help you overcome any nerves with a positive, affirmative introduction. Nerves can freeze our brains and leave us tongue-tied.

2. Have a Conversation

After making introductions, don't launch into a sales pitch. Have a conversation, one in which you ask open-ended questions and listen twice as much as you speak.

Open-ended questions will prompt the customer to start talking. It is exactly what you would do with a favorite relative: "Hi, Melissa, how are you? What was your vacation like? Tell me all! I can't wait to hear about it." Most salespeople use closed questions that result in a yes or no answer, like "Can I help you?" or "Are you interested?" Asking closed questions gives the customer the option of shutting down the conversation with a no answer.

The difference between an open and a closed question is the difference between asking "Did you like your vacation?" and asking "What was your vacation like?" Open questions ask for an explanation and prompt someone to engage in dialogue. Open questions often start with *what, why,* and *how.* For instance, in a clothes store, a sales assistant might ask a customer, "Can I help you?" and the customer can easily decline. But if the assistant asks, "What color tops do you prefer wearing?" it's harder to say, "No, thanks," without appearing rude, so most people will continue the conversation. You are not trying to trick the person. Instead, you are like a counselor trying to help the person solve their problem.

Then, once a customer responds, listen twice as much as you speak. Listening is the number-one selling skill. Everything your customer says gives you an opportunity to respond with another open-ended question. You can't do that if you are the one talking. Here's an example:

Business owner: What sort of tops are you looking for today?

Customer: Oh, I am just browsing, thanks. I'm not sure.

Business owner: Well, we just got a whole new line in the store. What is the occasion you are thinking of?

Customer: Oh, just a cocktail party my husband wants me to go to.

Business owner: That sounds like fun. Tell me more about the occasion.

Now you understand the customer's need, and you are there to help. You have struck up a natural conversation, and as the customer describes the event, you will probably get inspired ideas of what to show her to wear. Keep asking her for more specifics about what she likes, and then give her several options and honest feedback on her choices. What is so hard or intimidating about that? Yet whenever I am in a clothing store with my wife, I hear the same useless closed questions like "Can I help you?"

When we get nervous in front of a customer, we tend to think of our next question rather than listening to what the customer is saying. If you get nervous, one trick is to repeat back to the customer what they just said. This confirms you heard correctly and gives your brain time to digest the information and create a follow-up question. Here's a longer example:

Business owner: Thank you for your patience waiting. What brings you to our store today?

Customer: I bought this phone from your assistant last week, but the battery is dead all the time.

Business owner: You bought the phone here last week, but the battery is not working? [*Customer nods.*] I'm sorry you are having trouble. My name is John, and I'll be happy to assist you. May I ask your name?

Customer: Marybeth Lewis.

Business owner: Marybeth, let me pull up your purchase details. Before you used it, how long did you initially charge the phone?

Customer: No one told me I had to.

Business owner: I'm sorry, that must be the problem. It's our fault. We should have made that clear. The battery needs to be fully charged for a whole day before use. If not, this particular battery will never charge properly. I can offer two options. One is to replace the battery free of charge, or I could upgrade you to a phone that has a more sophisticated battery that can be used right away. What is your pattern of phone use?

Customer: Well, I use it all the time. I do just about everything on it.

Business owner: The battery you have, which comes standard with that phone, is okay for occasional use, but if you use your phone a lot, you would be better off with a battery that lasts several hours between charges. Since we messed up, I can offer you a deep discount on the more sophisticated phone. They normally retail at sixty dollars. How does thirty dollars sound, and you can use your phone as soon as you leave the store. [*Pause.*] Would you prefer this silver one or black?

3. Close the Sale

The final question above is an example of how to close a sale. You can also ask an open-ended question that encourages the customer to make a purchase or further the sales process: "What is your preferred color of phone?"

The customer might say, "I like silver," or "I'll just take a replacement battery," but either way, you've solved their problem successfully.

You don't need to be a master salesperson to succeed. You just need the courage and confidence to believe that you do the best work, or have the best product, and therefore, you have a right to ask the customer for their business and payment. All the marketing you do is useless unless you ask for the sale. Sales-technique gurus make "closing" seem mystical and difficult. It is, however, remarkably straightforward. You take a deep breath, open your mouth, and speak. To me, the easiest closing technique is to use what I call an "action close." That is, you simply request for another step in the sales process:

Business owner: It is a self-setting alarm clock, which means that all you have to do is plug it in, and when it asks what time you want to wake up, just tell it. Simple. No manual to read, no time wasted with fiddly knobs. We just got a new shipment, so right now we have every color in stock. Which color would you prefer?

Business owner: To help convince you to use my landscape service, I'd be pleased to take you to a similar project I completed only last year. It is nearby. If you have ten minutes tomorrow around the same time, I'll pick you up. Should we do that?

Business owner: What concerns do you have that would prevent you from ordering?

Business owner: If you place an order now, I can give you a 10 percent discount. What size do you prefer?

Business owner: I stand behind my product. If you are not completely satisfied, bring it back for a full refund. I have offered that guarantee the whole time I have been in business and have yet to give back a cent. In fact, when you refer me to your friends and family, if they mention your name, I will give them a 10 percent discount as well. How many would you like?

Business owner: It looks great on you. Your family and friends will all want one when they see it. I'll tell you what I can do. If you buy two now, I'll add a third for free, and you can give it to someone as a gift. What is the best size for you and the person you have in mind?

Outsourcing Direct Sales

Your product or service may eventually be best promoted with face-to-face sales activity, otherwise known as direct sales. There are many companies that offer syndicated/shared sales forces or lease options with a variety of configurations to fit your budget. Rather than pay for the cost of a dedicated sales-person for your product, it might make more sense to join a contract sales force that already promotes a couple of products to your target audience.

In these cases, you pay a reduced price for being one of several to be detailed, but if the other products have been around a while, you often find the salesperson speaks about the latest product first, so as to get more time and interest from prospects. You will also get lots of valuable market feedback, which can be worth the investment in itself.

All of the administration and people management is done by the company that owns the sales force, but if you have limited sales experience yourself, it will be hard for you to direct them. You still need to get out and sell to some people so that you can gather sufficient feedback about resistance and objections that the salespeople might face. Salespeople hate surprises when they are interacting with customers. Here are the main advantages for outsourcing salespeople:

- Cash-flow management. Add contracted salespeople as demand dictates, and treat marketing as a variable cost. If demand is so great that you have to scramble to get more salespeople, it is a high-quality problem to have, and this is far better than having to cut back, which always hurts morale.
- Human resources management and administration are handled by the vendor, which frees you up to run your business.
- Salespeople usually have established customer relationships, so your product "hits the ground running" without you having to create leads.
- Outsource companies have the latest technology to offer real-time analysis of the effectiveness of your marketing messages.

Most contract sales organizations also offer a menu of support services that can include dedicated or shared field sales teams, specialist sales services, marketing campaigns, and telesales. Contracts are customized to fit product needs and client budgets, and the contracting process will include decisions about the representative profile, the training program, management direction, the IT platform, and incentive plans.

Another use for contracted sales support is when you can't be in two places at once. For instance, if you have two overlapping trade shows at which you could exhibit your product, outsourced sales teams can offer short-term contracts to help you out.

Outsourced telesales offers a full range of outbound and inbound telesales options to promote products and services to decision makers over the phone, including product detailing, remote territory coverage, and vacant territory management. There are lots of companies that offer telesales services, and they can be expensive. Choose one that offers the following:

- Simple ROI measurement tools and real-time reporting
- Pay-on-performance option, so you only pay for results
- Free trial period to prove their value
- History of low staff turnover
- References from clients in the same sector as your company
- Comprehensive staff training

Finally, I would caution you to start slow with outsourced sales. We all have a tendency to hype our own ideas, and expectations for orders can be unrealistically high. Where possible, negotiate trial periods with the contract sales company, or hire only a few people to concentrate on a single area. Then test the results and confirm the return on investment before expanding.

Affiliate Marketing

Affiliate marketing is mostly an online practice. It uses a network of established retailers and their products to sell to a customer base in exchange for rewards or commissions. Behind the curtain of the website, software at each of the companies determines when the customer purchases through a certain website, and commissions get paid appropriately for the referral.

There are good and bad sides to affiliate marketing. The bad side is that many companies, entrepreneurs, and groups don't know or care about the quality of the products they advertise through their website banners. Authenticity is essential in every aspect of a business, and you should only include banners for companies that you have worked with and for products that have satisfied your needs over time.

The advantage of affiliate marketing is that it helps a startup company manage cash flow, and your company only has to pay when a product or service is sold. Affiliate marketing takes the expense of marketing and turns it into a cost of sale or a cost of goods sold. Affiliate programs are one of the most powerful online marketing tools available. Rather than paying out a lot of money and hoping that marketing works, you only pay out money when you know that it has worked.

There are four primary ways to locate affiliate programs for a target website:

1. Review affiliate program directories, which you can find by placing that phrase in any search engine.
2. Approach large affiliate networks.
3. Investigate the target website itself. Websites that offer an affiliate program often have a link in the footer or the "About" section of the website.
4. Find someone who is equally passionate about what you want to fix and who has a product that enhances yours and vice versa, and then cross-sell.

CHAPTER EIGHT

Winning Customers

Build a Trustworthy Relationship

*The aim of marketing is to know and understand the customer
so well the product or service fits him or her and sells itself.*
— PETER DRUCKER

When I first started a sales career, my trainers drummed into me the idea that "people buy people first." They instructed that no matter how good your product, if customers don't like you, they won't buy. The challenge is that people make their minds up about someone they meet in just a few seconds. We never get a second chance to make a great first impression.

Today the same adage applies to how people perceive you and your company from something as simple as landing on a website page. Studies show that it takes fifty milliseconds for someone to form an impression about a company or a product they see online. People tend not to buy from companies they don't like to be associated with or from people that make them uneasy. In my opinion, trustworthiness is now the most essential element in the purchase decision. When we trust a company, we are more likely to buy their offering. More importantly, we are more likely to recommend the company and offering to someone else.

This quality of trustworthiness is the end result of great marketing, which wins customers by cultivating a trustworthy relationship. As I discuss in chapter 7, customers pay attention to and care about not just the product itself but their entire interaction and experience with a business. This means paying attention to the company's image and making sure that every aspect of the customer's interaction is satisfying and makes them feel good.

The Recipe for Trustworthiness

What I like to call the "recipe for trustworthiness" is similar to what's called the "marketing mix." This is a blend of marketing tactics that encourages customers to buy. For decades, economists and marketers have spoken about this marketing mix in terms of the four Ps: product, price, promotion, and place (or distribution). When marketing a service, the four Ps are expanded to add: physical evidence (the store or web design), people (the employees who interact with customers), and process (the systems that impact marketing). In 1990, Robert Lauterborn proposed a four Cs classification that was more consumer oriented: consumer needs, cost, communication, and convenience.

The four Ps classification has become rather archaic for the way business is conducted today. It tends to encourage marketers to focus on the product rather than on the customer experience. Of course, great marketing must highlight the life-changing benefits of the product, but like Lauterborn, I think that the overall "marketing mix" should focus on the customer. Here are the five ingredients that I think make the ideal recipe and that together add up to the most important final product: authenticity through trustworthiness. The rest of this chapter explores them in detail.

1. **Make reasonable claims:** If you promise the moon, you must deliver the moon. When extolling the benefits of your product or service, don't overclaim. Customers are suspicious of exaggeration, and if a product or service doesn't live up to the hype, they'll be disappointed. Then you'll lose their trust, and they won't buy again.

2. **Create a trustworthy company image:** Create an image of your company that the customer trusts and is proud to be associated with. It is not enough to have fancy logos and business cards. You must appeal to your customer's emotions, their likes and dislikes.

3. **Set a fair price:** While your price must obviously cover your costs, the customer decides if that price is "fair," and this evaluation is complex. When making a purchasing decision, the customer considers the cost of switching from one product or service to another, the cost of shipping, the cost of paying by installments, the product's quality, the competition, and so on. When you get the package right, the customer receives the product or service as advertised, on time, for the cost anticipated, and you engender trust. If there are hidden costs or the product doesn't seem worth the price, you lose trust.

4. **Communicate professionally and respectfully:** Communication needs have changed dramatically. Under the old mix, great effort was made by the company to push information toward the potential customer. The new mix switches from push to pull. Your aim is to communicate respectfully and be open to feedback so

the customer feels valued. Make sure your communication involves give and take, like a real conversation, which engenders trust.

5. **Make purchasing easy:** The transaction itself should be as easy for the customer as possible. If the customer has to expend effort to make a purchase, they may decide it's too much trouble. This means providing accessible customer service to solve problems and handle upgrades.

Make Reasonable Claims

The first thing that all winning ideas and winning products must do is satisfy a customer need. Customers are a very needy group. Too often, marketing gets caught up extolling a product's superior features, but none of that matters if the product doesn't benefit the customer by solving their problems in the way they want them solved.

However, to engender trust, your product or service must live up to whatever promises your marketing makes. The temptation to oversell can be strong — to make the benefits seem even better, more amazing, and more life-changing than they really are. Avoid this. Too often customers are disappointed with the comparison between the product as advertised and the actual experience of it in their hands. If they are led to expect more, this can undermine the customer's genuine satisfaction with the actual benefits they experience. Today, it is better to underpromise and overdeliver, which creates pleasantly surprised and pleased customers, since their expectations have been exceeded. And those happy customers have the means to tell everyone else through social media. Unfortunately, so do dissatisfied customers.

This issue of expectations and needs is a bit of a chicken-and-egg debate. Steve Jobs famously said, "People don't know what they want until we show it to them." After all, when only radio existed, no one felt deprived. But as soon as television was invented, radio wasn't good enough anymore, and everyone suddenly "needed" a TV. In other words, customers may not necessarily expect certain benefits from your product, but if you promise those benefits, they will come to expect them, and they will hold it against you if the product doesn't deliver.

Create a Trustworthy Company Image

Harland Sanders was born on a small farm in Henryville, Indiana, in 1890. Following the death of his father in 1896, his mother worked two jobs and taught Harland to cook for his siblings in her place. Forced out by an abusive stepfather, Sanders left home and school when he was twelve years old to work as a farmhand for four dollars a month (ninety-five dollars in today's value). Over the next two decades, he did a variety of jobs, including painter, railroad firefighter, plowman, streetcar conductor, ferryboat operator, insurance salesperson, justice of the peace, and service station operator.

Proving the maxim that it is never too late to reinvent yourself, in 1929 Sanders opened a gas station in Corbin, Kentucky. He cooked for his family, and for an occasional customer in the back room, and his reputation traveled by word of mouth. He enjoyed cooking the food his mother had taught him to make when he was a small child: pan-fried chicken, country ham, fresh vegetables, and homemade biscuits. Demand for Sanders's cooking rose, and it became his more lucrative business. Eventually, he moved across the street to a facility with a 142-seat restaurant, a motel, and a gas station.

During the 1930s, the world-renowned image of an avuncular colonel developed. First, the state's governor named Sanders an honorary Kentucky colonel. Then Sanders developed a unique method of spicing and pressure-frying chicken. Due to its regional popularity, the Harland Sanders Court and Café received an endorsement by Duncan Hines's *Adventures in Good Eating* in 1939.

In 1952, the colonel, then sixty-two, signed on his first franchise to Pete Harman, who owned a hamburger restaurant in Salt Lake City. For the next four years, he persuaded several other restaurant owners to add his "Kentucky fried chicken" to their menus. In 1955, Sanders incorporated his company, and the following year he took his chicken recipe on the road, doing demonstrations on-site to sell his method. Clad in a white suit, white shirt, and black string tie, sporting a white mustache and goatee, and carrying a cane, Sanders dressed in a way that expressed his energy and enthusiasm, and he created a company image that lived long in customers' memories. By 1963 Sanders's recipe was franchised to more than six hundred outlets in the United States and Canada.

In 1964, refusing to accept aging or retirement, Sanders sold Kentucky Fried Chicken for $2 million and a per-year salary of $40,000 for public appearances; that salary later rose to $200,000. The offer came from an investor group headed by John Y. Brown Jr., a twenty-nine-year-old graduate of the University of Kentucky law school, and by Nashville financier John Massey. A notable member of the investor group was Pete Harman, who had been the first to purchase Sanders's recipe twelve years earlier, and he believed he could market the image.

Meanwhile, Harland Sanders enjoyed his less hectic role as roving ambassador. In *Business Week*, Massey remarked: "He's the greatest PR image I have ever known."

This story exemplifies the perfect company image. The avuncular, distinguished "colonel" (trustworthy) wants only to satisfy your needs by providing tasty and comfortable food (trust again), which is offered in a convenient package and lo-cation at a price that makes the purchase decision easy (value also equals trust).

In some fashion, you want your company to evoke the same trustworthy image as Colonel Sanders: respected, skillful, well-intentioned, and wanting to help others. Colonel Sanders was a real person, but he became a symbol who, in a single image, embodied all the trustworthy attributes a company wants to represent. This is why spokespeople can be very effective in marketing. However, you don't need to become or invent a "character." You just need to make sure all the elements of your company's image evoke expertise, reassurance, care, and trust.

Today, technology makes it easy to create websites, logos, and business cards for a small investment. For startups using the hub model, with no office or storefront, these things will convey the image that customers encounter. That said, remember that trustworthiness and company image are about more than a logo. It involves all the attributes discussed in this chapter and elsewhere, such as what happens when a customer calls the number on your great-looking business card. Will your teenage daughter answer the shared house/business phone and shout for you from the hall? It sounds obvious, but we have all been on the end of those mistakes.

Here are four of the main image tools at your disposal: company logo, company address, business cards, and website.

Company Logo

Once you've chosen a company name (see "What Is Your Company Name?" pages 37–38), you need an eye-catching logo. However, don't sweat this any more than you should worry about your company name. Your main focus is to create exceptional products and services, so the purpose of the logo is for it to be simple, attractive, and professional. Nothing more, nothing less. Do not lie awake at night worrying about it.

For my first company, I designed my own logo from a program that came free with my laptop in 2003 (the company still has that logo), but I do not recommend you do the same. Professionally made logos can be purchased online for less than thirty dollars. Here are some design suggestions to keep in mind:

- Word logos are boring, and it is hard to stand out from well-known ones like Google and Yahoo. Choose an image that creates a sense of activity and movement. A useful tool is to type something about your company or product into a search engine, and then click on images when the results arrive. What shows up can help inspire your logo ideas.
- Add a short tagline that describes your business or product. The tagline should not say what the product is, but it should name what need it satisfies or what customer benefit it offers.
- A little color goes a long way and attracts attention. According to the psychology of color, blue is associated with trust and peace.
- Consider transferability. Because the logo will go on all your stationery, product packages, and so on, it needs to be easily transferable. Keep images simple, use standard fonts, and use only one to three common colors.

Company Address

By definition, the company location for a home-based, virtual startup is your home. There is no separate physical place of business. However, the world around you values real estate, which is concrete and reassuring, and an upscale, glitzy address conveys status and accomplishment. Conversely, a "virtual" business can be devalued and dismissed as barely existing. The challenge for you is to appear as anything but a home-based startup. Customers and clients make instant judgments, and right away, you want your enterprise to appear seasoned (even though it is not) and successful (even though it is not *yet*).

Don't use your home address for your business. This will be judged, and it will likely convey an image of instability or inexperience. Instead, get a mailbox service that offers an impressive-sounding address; lots of companies provide this. Avoid PO boxes because they generally don't accept courier mail, and they also don't improve your image. I selected an address in a well-known business area, and after putting the address on my business card and stationery, people said to me, "My! You must be doing really well to have an office there." In reality, it was just a mail-forwarding service that cost a few dollars a month.

Business Cards

These days, good-quality business cards are inexpensive to make. There is no need to spend more than a few dollars. However, do not print homemade cards because they look...well, homemade. Then, in terms of shape and design, avoid anything too gimmicky. You want your customers to keep the card in their file or wallet, not hand it around to others because it is funny or odd shaped.

A business card is more than a piece of hard-pressed paper with contact data. It is often the first or only impression a client or customer gets of your business. It can also be the most powerful sales tool in your arsenal.

Effective sales techniques engage a potential customer or client in conversation. Dialogue leads to interest. Interest leads to inquiries. Inquiries lead to sales. Business cards are an easy way to start the process with just about anyone, since they allow you to initiate a conversation. Here are the key design elements:

- Your combination of logo, tagline, and address create the entire company image you need, so you do not need to complicate the card. This aspect should cover less than half of one side.
- The front of the card *must* mention your main product or service and a benefit for the customer. For instance: "Quality. No compromises."
- Keep the design clear and simple. Cluttered cards give an impression of a disorganized company and make it difficult for the recipient to get the main message.
- Job title and qualifications: Some people suggest not adding job titles and qualifications. I understand the need to be humble, but this reduces your opportunities for opening up a conversation, which is the main point of a business card. People might ask questions about your degree or title. As for the job title, I prefer CEO, which implies a company with employees; whereas "president" or "owner" imply a small business run by one person. As for qualifications, add them only if noteworthy and relevant, such as MD, PhD, or MBA. Remember, you create trust by making reasonable claims, about yourself *and* your product.
- Always use a card material that can be written on. This may mean using a matte rather than a glossy design. Leave the reverse side mostly blank. In business, the reverse side has been the drawing board for many a successful sale. It makes an excellent place to write quick quotes or present a concept.
- Whatever your card design, make sure it includes easy contact information, such as a toll-free number and website address.

Website

There is no excuse for an amateurish or cluttered website, and even less of an excuse for having no website at all. No matter what your product or service, people expect to find a website to check you out. That is one way they use their senses to get a gut feel for who you are and to develop essential trustworthiness.

A few years ago, I purchased a house that was only partly finished. The builder gave me a list of all the subcontractors who had worked on the house until then, such as electricians, plumbers, and carpenters. When I went online to check them out, I found that only four out of twenty subcontractors had a website, and two of those sites looked amateurish.

I found excellent alternatives to everyone on the list. Some months later, some of the original vendors showed up and asked me why I had not continued with their services. I said they did not have websites, and I don't have the time to call everyone and get to know them. They argued that websites are expensive to set up and time-consuming to maintain. The opposite is true.

Despite the simplicity of setting up a website, and gaining access to potential online commerce worth more than $1 trillion, recent studies have found that less than two-thirds of small businesses have a website, though half of those without a website say they plan to build one. And yet, more than a quarter of small businesses with a website spend less than five hundred dollars on it. That seems to me a bit like leasing a store and refusing to dress the window. I am sure that all the survey respondents, whether they have a business website or not, immediately start searching online and clicking on websites when *they* need a service or product. It makes no sense in today's commercial world to avoid having a website.

I suggest that not only does every company need a website, but every company needs a high-quality and eye-catching one.

Just having a website is no longer enough. Not having a website at all is plain dumb when it is so easy to get one and so many people go online.

As I mention, people form an impression of a website within fifty milliseconds, or faster than the blink of an eye. All the money you spend on marketing can be wasted if your website turns them off or does not compel customers to linger. So who better to guide you than customers? Get their feedback frequently and redesign your website until they say they like it. As an example, check out my website: www.trevorgblake.com. I am very proud of it, since it reflects both my personality and my mission. The total investment, including membership sites and functionality, to build it was around $7,000. The website took several months to build because I took time with the developers to explain and focus my brand — an image or positioning that reflects one's core values, something developers call an "avatar."

Think of your website as a real store, and make sure that the first impression for a potential customer is great. They need to feel wanted and appreciated for stopping by. Then, give them something to do or investigate — some reason to click on something. In a real store, you might offer free samples as people step through the door. On my website, I offer a free twenty-seven-page download about the brain benefits of sticking to a five-hour workday. In a cyber store, perhaps offer a short inspiring video, a free newsletter, or an ebook to view, but what you offer must have value and provide the surfer an authentic benefit. In doing so you are showing the potential customer that you value his or her interest. You have no idea whether the person browsing your site has one dollar or a million dollars to spend, so imagine every visitor is rich, and design everything to attract them.

Getting a professional, eye-catching website set up is easy

and inexpensive, and there are countless online services to choose from. Having no website at all will immediately lose a customer's trust, since they may assume you have something to hide or that you don't really stand behind your product or service.

Set a Fair Price

When developing your business plan, you must figure out a price for your product or service. However, setting a price is more complicated than simply adding up your costs per item and then adding on top whatever net profit you want to make. As with everything in business, we must look through the eyes of the customer and take into account all their calculations about what makes a "fair price" for what you're selling, and their calculation has little to do with how much it costs to produce what you make. At the end of the day, price your product as high as the market will bear, and the only way to determine that is by asking customers.

Price and demand are forever bedfellows. With cyber sales and shipping options, however, we also must consider the cost of getting the product delivered or installed. We also have to make allowances for the costs of handling, payment terms, transaction fees, credit-card fees, marketing, warehousing, and overhead.

For example, when making a purchasing decision for a phone, the customer will consider the price of the phone, the length and terms of the rate plan, the package of services on offer, the ease of upgrading as better phones come along, and the time and effort of setting up the phone. The customer will also take into account how easy it is to get the phone and which company has the strongest signal in their location. Those are a lot of considerations for a single purchase decision, but customers make these formulas in their heads and take into account their own priorities.

The company selling the phone has to anticipate what matters to customers and attempt to make every element that they can control cost-effective and convenient. Your price must seem "fair" based on the customer's calculation (which admittedly isn't always logical). That changes the way phones would have been priced a couple of decades ago. Then it would have been more about the cost of manufacturing and distribution to the store plus a service and handling charge. It was a simpler formula, and the customer was not as involved in the decision.

Today, you have to think like a customer and offer prices and packages for a variety of budgets, while still keeping decisions as simple as possible. Too many choices can be as bad as too few.

Communicate Professionally and Respectfully

Every time you communicate with customers or clients, you have an opportunity to create an image and build trust. While any direct communication is obviously an opportunity to advertise your product or service again, you also want to build a relationship. Whether you write to someone, speak on the phone, or use social media, every time you communicate with customers or clients, you have the opportunity to reassure them that they have made a good purchasing decision while inviting another one. You might never get another chance to communicate with them.

Written Etiquette

All forms of written communication offer a marketing opportunity, such as brochures, letters, invoices, proposals, emails, texts, Facebook pages, Twitter messages, and whatever new communication tool comes next. Never miss the chance to remind recipients about your product or service, how it benefits them, how they can get more information, and how grateful you are for their business.

Every week I get sloppy communication from people who own small businesses. I get emails in which the owner signs off with just initials or leaves the smartphone's default signature intact; texts that have no product or contact information on them; and plain invoices devoid of logo, marketing message, or tantalizing offers. All of them are wasted opportunities to create a company image or attract another sale. Here are some things to keep in mind:

- **Invoices:** Offer discounts on another purchase or rewards for referring customers to a website via a traceable code.
- **Device texts:** Change the default tagline such as "sent via my Xphone" to a recognizable signature that includes company name, product name, and website link to the product information.
- **Solicitation emails:** Use short, active subject lines with positive verbs like "Learn," "Download," "Earn," or "Sign Up." Never use ALL CAPS. Avoid words that junk filters harvest, such as "offer" or "credit." Always sign off professionally with a full contact-information block and links to business-related social media pages.

Telephone Etiquette

First impressions count, and many times the first real contact a potential customer has with you is from a phone call. In a virtual company, that call often comes directly to you as the owner of the business, and your skill as a communicator is what will create a sense of trustworthiness.

However, as I mention in chapter 6 (see "Telephone Setup," pages 166–67), you may want to hire a virtual call center to give the impression of a larger organization, and you certainly must have a dedicated phone line for the business, separate from your home phone. Whatever options you choose, the goal is to present your company in a professional, customer-oriented manner so that prospects gain a sense of confidence that allows them to base their purchasing decision upon the issues that are important — not on how big you are or how many people work for you.

Whatever positions entrepreneurs held in their previous jobs, I always suggest mimicking the friendly, professional manners of a typical corporate receptionist when answering the phone and for voicemail and attendant services. It is not unusual for me to call a business owner and receive a gruff grunt of a greeting. That does not portray a quality company image or a company that appreciates the fact that I am taking the time to call.

Many years ago I learned the benefit of speaking a formal greeting when answering the phone, such as: "Good morning, this is Trevor. How may I help you?" It is amazing how positively people respond to this friendly, open question. When I first started doing that, it sounded odd to me because I am not normally that open and friendly, but with a bit of practice, it became quite natural.

On my voicemail message, I make a point to thank the caller for making the effort to contact me. Such small, positive statements can make a huge impact on your company image. A typical message could be as follows:

Hello, you have reached [company name], the makers of [mention your product, service, or tagline]. We [never "I," to convey the image of a larger company] are sorry that we are busy helping another client right now [never "away from my desk"]. Please leave a message after the tone. We check voicemail frequently, and someone *will* return your call. Thank you for calling us at [company name].

Many phone service companies offer professional voicemail and customized attendant messages, all for very little cost compared to the benefit. To lose even a single customer because of an amateurish telephone greeting response is inexcusable today.

Social Media Etiquette

In 2018, 47 percent of small-business owners spent less than $10,000 on digital marketing, and 71 percent of owners did it all themselves instead of using experts. One in ten didn't invest in any kind of marketing, and one in five didn't use digital marketing at all.

I am a bit of a dunce at social media. Just like my first homemade website, my initial social media efforts were amateurish and portrayed a poor image of my company. I learned a harsh lesson and thereafter hired digital marketing experts.

Because I am always curious about every business function, I also pestered them to educate me as they performed various tasks. This is just another cross-function training necessity for the single-person startup. That meant they needed to show me the "backend" of advertising giants like Facebook and Google. I still don't know exactly what a "backend" is beyond various coding languages to achieve different networking tasks, but I get that social media is all about connecting you and your offering with like-minded people...potential buyers, in other words. I was, however, astonished at the capability of social media to segment markets and target customers with a higher likelihood to be attracted to the benefits of my books and courses. These are people with needs looking for exactly the kind of solutions I provide.

Through their work I realized that the typical business owner like me understands the depth and capability of social media marketing about as well as a polar bear understands the depth of the ice it stands on.

Like all marketing efforts, social media is very time-consuming, and also requires specific skills. Doing it yourself at the outset might not be the wisest choice when you have so many other things to do. You have to build an audience. You have to turn them into a community. You have to get that community really focused on and interested in what you want to talk about. Then once they believe in you, once they see that you're on their side, you can put things in front of them that might be of use. If you have the skills to do that, then by all means go for it, but if you are more like me, think about hiring experts who can provide you and your business with the best tools. Then you can focus on growth or new products and offerings.

Social media is also a rapid-feedback, two-way channel. If you listen carefully to the chatter your community radiates, it can help you enhance your product and service. The goal of any company is to satisfy customer needs, so you have to listen well. For me, that is the main benefit of having a social media platform. It provides a real-time measurement of what your customers think of you.

One risk with social media, along with any communication style that involves truncated messages, is engaging in sloppy communication that is easy to misinterpret. Avoid trying to speak like your audience, as this comes over as inauthentic and even condescending. No matter how much you want to say, always leave a way for the recipient to click onto a link that takes them to a website. Less is more.

Finally, as I mention in chapter 7, carefully evaluate the return on investment for any paid social media campaign. This can be hard to calculate and not very high, especially for a low-cost consumable product. Make sure you have a good understanding of conversion rates before you jump into the game. Different sources claim different conversion rates, but 3 percent is typically quoted for Facebook and Google. If your product is low cost, that rate makes it difficult to get a return on investment in social media marketing. If, however, your product costs several thousand dollars, then a 3 percent return is very attractive.

Make Purchasing Easy

I started my first business at the age of twelve when I used to take a bus to and from school. After picking up a dozen unruly kids from school, the bus would make a stop in town to pick up day shoppers. Because the adult passengers paid fares, and these were the days of handing over cash and receiving change, the stop would last about ten minutes while transactions took place. Immediately behind the bus stop was a candy store. Kids were tempted to jump off the bus to buy candy, but no one dared take the risk of missing the bus departure from the stop. The driver was surly and would not have cared about stranding any kids.

I grew up poor and did not get an allowance, so I could not afford any candy. On the way to the stop, I collected orders for candy along with appropriate payment from my fellow unruly kids. As soon as the bus stopped and the door opened, I leapt onto the sidewalk and ran into the candy shop. While the shoppers were paying for their fare and taking a seat, I bought the candy. It was always tricky timing, but I never missed the bus. When I returned to the bus, I distributed the candy in exchange for a commission of a couple of candies from each client.

I learned two important business lessons. The first is that eating your profits is not a smart way to grow a company (and it is also bad for your teeth). The second is that people happily pay a premium for convenience, which in this case meant not having to risk missing the bus ride home.

Convenience from a marketing perspective means making it easy and worry-free for the customer to make a purchase decision. A product on its own might be the best quality and value available, but if the seller does not offer simple delivery options, easy and free installation, setup support, and easy payment options, a customer might choose a competitive but lesser product because it is more conveniently packaged. This does not mean giving add-on values away for free. People are usually happy to pay a higher price for convenience.

Then, when making a sale, you also need to get paid quickly so that revenue flows in quickly. Through your website and customer-service function, you need to offer the same options as even the largest retailers. Whatever payment systems you choose, you need to keep up with trends and use whatever customers prefer, or whatever is easiest and most popular with them. I still come across business owners who don't take credit card payments, and others who don't have an automated online payment system, so they require me to write a check. Writing a check is inconvenient to me, so I will shop elsewhere.

Here are the main online payment systems:

- **ACH payments** are electronic credit and debit transfers, allowing customers to make payments from their bank accounts. ACH stands for *automated clearing house,* and most payment processors offer ACH payment options to their customers, especially for monthly and subscription-based transactions. Most payment solutions use ACH to send money (minus fees) to their customers.

- **A merchant account** is a bank account that allows a merchant to receive customer payments through credit or debit cards. Merchant providers are required to obey regulations established by card associations. Many processors act as both the merchant account and the payment gateway.

- **A payment gateway** allows merchants to securely pass credit card information between the customer and the merchant and also between the merchant and the payment processor or bank. The payment gateway is the middleman between the merchant and the sponsoring bank.

- **A payment processor** is the company that a merchant uses to handle credit card transactions. Payment processors implement antifraud measures to ensure that both the front-facing customer and the merchant are protected. Ideally, make sure the payment environment is PCI compliant, or that it follows the security standards established by the Payment Card Industry (PCI) Security Standards Council.

Lots of specialist companies exist to help small businesses set up payment options (just search online). There will be a small setup fee and a small commission for each transaction. It is well worth those commissions in exchange for getting paid quickly, and you can configure the costs into your price.

CHAPTER NINE

The Success Mentality

*Like it or not, there is a thing that can be called the
Millionaire Mentality. There is a frame of mind, which puts
an individual a long way ahead on the road to success.
In short, the Millionaire Mentality is one which is always
and above all cost-conscious and profit-minded.*

— J. Paul Getty

In order to cultivate the creative mindset to conceive of a winning idea, I suggest making a routine of meditation and experiencing nature, along with embracing the power of the feminine (which I describe in chapter 1). Then, to thrive as an ongoing business, I suggest cultivating "the success mentality." This isn't just one mindset but a collection of attitudes that, when properly balanced, add up to a winning approach to growing your business. This starts by cultivating both adaptability and discipline, but it also includes embracing leadership, always focusing on the customer and continuous improvement, and having fun.

The Adaptability Mentality

Adaptability is a key trait of successful entrepreneurs. Today, that doesn't just mean openness to change, but the ability to adapt fast enough to keep up with rapid changes in customer needs, markets, and technology. As I've said, traditional corporate structures and approaches hamper adaptability in our information age, and even once-great companies can now become extinct in the time it takes to assemble a team of people to study a problem, collect the data, and reach a consensus about what to do.

An excellent example is Circuit City, which Jim Collins wrote about in his book *Good to Great*. For decades, Circuit City was the number-two electronics retailer in the United States, but it filed for bankruptcy protection in late 2008, blaming a slowdown in consumer spending. That is something failed companies often say. The failure was not due to the company or its inflexible decision-making. It was consumers' fault because they preferred to shop somewhere else. How dare they!

"Circuit City was incredibly successful in the 1980s and 1990s, but they never changed after that," said David Schick, an analyst at Stifel Nicolaus, in *Time* magazine, which commented: "If it had adapted, it might have ended up like its chief rival, Best Buy, which in August [2008] reported both increased sales and a quarterly profit of $200 million. Instead, Circuit City reported a loss of $239 million in late September."

Documentaries show how the founders of Circuit City — the Wurtzel Family — treated their employees almost like family and involved them in the decision-making process. There was no formal hierarchy, only a lean management structure with people empowered to decide. That culture requires an element of trust because deciding on the spot often means using intuition as much as analysis.

As the company grew exponentially, however, more and

more management layers were introduced, and the voices of employees got filtered out. Senior management became too distant from the sales floor, where feedback about trends and customer preferences are gathered. Things started to take a negative turn when the company hired a new CEO who had absolutely no interest in the expertise or instincts of his employees. He felt that knowledgeable employees were a costly item on the balance sheet. He fired almost 3,500 experienced employees immediately and replaced them with inexperienced minimum-wage staff. It was an error from which the company never recovered.

On a smaller scale, I recently came across a startup company that had just a few weeks of cash left. Most of the employees had been let go, and a skeleton crew of four senior managers worked in a huge, empty office building. The company possessed a technology it no longer used, but one that I felt could fit well into one of my projects. Respecting the company's dire cash situation, I made a reasonable offer so management could receive cash immediately and the company would be guaranteed to survive a few months more — perhaps long enough to secure the additional funding it needed.

I thought it was a no-brainer, and the transaction could have been completed in twenty-four hours. Instead, it took management two weeks just to find a date for us to meet. I lived only a few miles away and was available any day. After we finally met, they held a private meeting to discuss the proposal and then took another two weeks before they called me with a decision to move ahead.

I emailed them a contract I have used a half-dozen times with much larger outfits. They hired a lawyer to wordsmith the clauses, which went on for weeks before I got so frustrated that I walked away from the deal. Their company went bankrupt a month later.

By the terms of the company's intellectual-property contracts, the technology I was interested in returned to the inventor, who ran a single-person company. I contacted him the following day, and within twenty-four hours we had agreed on a deal and executed a contract.

Rare is the company that empowers its employees to take ownership of an issue and make decisions. Like the original Circuit City, they do exist, and other examples are Wegmans, the Apple Store, and the Ritz-Carlton hotel chain, all of which have reputations of excellence in customer care and customer loyalty. Other companies contact them regularly to learn their secrets, and in a 2012 *Forbes* article, the companies claimed the secret for their success with customer loyalty is that they empower employees to make on-the-spot decisions.

Adaptability Balances Intuition *and* Analysis

Many startup entrepreneurs are indoctrinated in the old way of thinking that prizes analysis over intuition and consensus over empowerment. Most large companies respond to an unexpected business issue by calling a meeting of peers, employees, and supervisors to discuss it, and then only acting if consensus is reached. But quick decisions often have to be made in the absence of all facts or data; they require a mixture of logic and intuition. And adaptability can mean forgoing the corporate decision-by-committee approach and empowering all employees with the ability to act.

Culturally, logic or analysis is often considered a masculine trait, and intuition is a feminine trait. All people possess both, but studies have shown that men have a tendency to prefer analysis and mistrust their intuition, while women have more permission to use their intuition, and so they rely on it and trust it more often. Just as often, these attributes are considered at odds or even mutually exclusive, but I believe that successful, adaptable decision-making comes from balancing analysis of data and trusting what our intuition tells us. Call it yin and yang, or male and female energy, it matters not. In order to survive and succeed in business, we all need to gather hard data and a variety of opinions as much as possible to analyze the market as accurately as possible. Yet we also need to trust our instincts, and the instincts of our employees, when we sense danger (like competitive threats) and opportunities (like customer preferences) even in the absence of hard data.

For the modern entrepreneur, the adaptability mentality requires balance. Too much focus on analysis and consensus can be paralyzing. Yet if someone simply flies by the seat of their pants, ignoring all data, then chaos can ensue; actions can lack focus, coherence, and effectiveness. Achieving balance helps you learn to trust your instincts while also verifying with data that what you believe is actually occurring.

Here are several things you can do to foster balance and improve your ability to make better, quicker decisions:

- Get cross-function experience (see pages 137–41) in as many areas as possible, which improves confidence in being able to understand issues and their implications. It provides fuel for your intuition.
- Develop a regular meditation practice (see pages 16–19). Some of the scientifically proven benefits of daily meditation are improved intuition and the ability to create more accurate solutions to problems.
- In a startup using the hub model, build close relationships with the client managers or representatives at all your vendors. Vendors focus on your company's markets, and they have a front-row seat for trends and changes. However, they will care enough about your company to call you when they see something good

or bad happening only if you have already developed strong bonds.

- Create a culture of empowerment within your virtual company. Permit vendors and their customer-service personnel to make decisions on your behalf. This takes courage. *Empowerment* is an overused word, and few managers I have met are hands-off personalities. Most are closer to being control freaks. Of course, you provide vendors with overall direction, but in a virtual model, you do not have the luxury of walking down the office hallway to check on everyone's progress. For vendors, one attraction of being a contracted worker is autonomy, or being free to work without close supervision. Hire good vendors, and then trust the people you hire to make smart decisions without micromanaging.
- Consider gender balance in hiring — whether of vendors, contractors, or employees — since there is overwhelming evidence of the benefits of a balanced male/female ratio in leadership (see pages 13–16). This helps ensure a balance of aptitudes and attitudes among those people helping you run your business.

The Discipline Mentality

In "The Importance of Self-Confidence" (pages 47–48), I mention the famous study of 1,528 gifted children with genius-level IQs. Self-confidence was one of two main ingredients that differentiated the successful from the not-so-successful children, and the other was discipline. Together, discipline and self-confidence are critical foundations of the success mentality. What exactly is a discipline mentality?

Mary Kay Wagner Ash never finished college. She worked

for a variety of direct sales companies, where she rose through the ranks. Rejected for promotion in favor of a young man whom she had helped train, she chose to take her destiny into her own hands. At that time she was forty-five years old.

She started writing a book designed to help young women navigate through a male-dominated business world. Before she knew it, her unfinished book transformed into a business plan. It was 1963, and gloomy economic forecasts predicted a downturn (one that never materialized), and a month before she started her company, Mary Kay's second husband died.

Undeterred, she invested her entire life savings of $5,000 and recruited the help of her son, who eventually became the company's executive chairman. She hired nine freelance consultants, who all worked out of their homes, and then she opened her first store in Dallas. At that time her company was called Beauty by Mary Kay.

Today, Mary Kay Cosmetics is a recognized brand all over the world, and in 2014, global revenue exceeded $3 billion. In her autobiography, *The Mary Kay Way*, she outlines what it takes for a beauty consultant to succeed and highlights the importance of discipline as a tool for the successful entrepreneur.

She repeats this advice in her two motivational books *Mary Kay on People Management* (1984) and *Mary Kay — You Can Have It All* (1995). At length she describes the significance of discipline of mind and the importance of seemingly simple organizational skills like making lists. She shows validated data on how productivity and profit increase when businesspeople finish their day by writing a to-do list for the following day. She also demonstrates the difference in results between consultants who are disciplined in their follow-up procedures compared to those who are less so.

She wrote, "My list keeps me on track, and I give it all the credit when people tell me how well I follow up. I write down everything that requires follow-through, and once on paper, it becomes a tangible commitment that I must attend to."

What Mary Kay describes seems simple, and it is. No cutting-edge technology is involved. To write lists is hardly a new idea, and most people readily accept the value of them. Most people also often fail to apply this simple, everyday discipline to their business.

I know several small-business owners who never write anything down. They fool themselves into believing that they can remember everything. The result is late and often incorrect invoices, forgotten orders or promises, missed timelines, and frustrated clients. They do quality work, but the overall impression I get as a customer is less than satisfying because I end up having to chase them for forgotten matters.

I know others who go to the trouble of working out complicated quotes, but then forget to follow up in a timely manner with the prospective client. These same people also forget to send invoices for months, by which time I have trouble recalling what it is they are invoicing.

People sometimes confuse discipline with determination. Both are mental attitudes, but discipline is also a skill. If your habitual reaction is to write a note or a reminder to yourself, or to obsessively schedule everything, then you have the correct mentality. You don't need fancy devices. The most efficient person I have contracted with recently still uses a paper diary and pen. She never fails to double-check appointments a day before our meeting or to follow up with an action plan the day after. Consequently, I have recommended her to many others.

Discipline is an easy skill to master, and perhaps that is the problem. It is so easy that most people ignore it. A mentality of discipline is essential in your business, and there are two key areas to consider: task discipline and schedule discipline.

Task Discipline

Task discipline is about developing habits that get things done. This involves what are essentially four steps: Make a to-do list at the end of every day; do the first task at the start of every day; keep a separate list of follow-up tasks; and finish what you start.

- **Make a to-do list at the end of every day:** Further, prioritize that list, with the most important actions first. This will do two things. First, it helps relieve the stress and fear of forgetting something, and you'll be more relaxed in the evening. Your family will stop complaining about you being so distracted all the time. Second, by writing the list, you make a subtle commitment to perform the tasks. It is your disciplined commitment to ensure a productive day tomorrow.

- **Do the first task at the start of every day:** When you enter your work space the next day, review the list and start the first task immediately. This is an essential discipline. Do not be tempted to check emails, voicemail, or texts first, as they will scatter your focus in a hundred different directions. Get that first, most-important task done before you give in to the temptation to do anything else. This is particularly important if you conduct business across time zones and have to play catch-up with people whose day begins hours earlier. Even when you have half a day's communications to respond to, get the first task done before checking them and responding. Many biographies and self-help books give this advice. It is good and it works.

- **Keep a separate list of follow-up tasks:** Depending on your type of business, this may be less or more important. However, we all have the habit of making promises in the moment that we later struggle to remember. Since customer satisfaction is a top priority, whenever you make a promise, write the details on a follow-up list and schedule it on a calendar. Every day, review this list and follow up, as promised.

- **Finish what you start:** We have all experienced checking in to a hotel or airport, and the person helping us then takes a phone call. It is as if a wall is instantly erected. Although we still exist, we have suddenly become invisible to the receptionist. We become the person's unfinished task, and we are stuck and annoyed as a result. Most of us do this: When something interrupts our attention, we usually stop what we are doing and focus on the intrusion. This bad habit can be exacerbated when we work from home, since isolation and loneliness can lead us to seek distractions. Avoid this temptation. Don't drop what you are doing every time the phone rings or a new email arrives. Even quick distractions can cause us to lose focus, and then it takes more time to get back to the task at hand. Once you pick an important task from your to-do list, start it and finish it, without allowing any interruptions or distractions.

Schedule Discipline

In chapter 6, I discuss strategies and tips for working from home (see pages 154–60), and this can be one of the biggest challenges for entrepreneurs who are running a hub-model startup after a long career in a large company. At home, there is no set schedule, and creating and sticking to a schedule is no one's job but yours. This requires self-discipline and self-motivation in

general, but where that really counts is maintaining a productive, balanced schedule.

I asked Julie — a successful freelance consultant who spent
most of her working life in a regular office environment before
taking the home-based business plunge — about her experiences of schedules. This is what she shared:

> One of the biggest challenges is balance between per-
> sonal time and work schedule — which I will admit
> I haven't been able to perfectly achieve. I think there
> are two general categories of employees: either "self-
> motivated" or "slackers."
>
> If you know yourself to have a tendency toward the
> "slacker" mentality, I don't believe there is any point in
> attempting to work from home. I would say the slack-
> ers of the world are better off staying at an office where
> they've got someone playing the role of their "nagging
> parent" to monitor them and "keep them in line."
>
> For the "self-motivated" employee, the challenge is
> to be able to walk away from the work (which is just
> a room away, 24/7). I am happy to work, enjoy work-
> ing, and treasure the opportunity to do it from home...
> but at times it truly is hard to stop. Even if I do stop to
> attend to a personal task, once the task is done, I find
> my mind wandering back to thoughts of work items I
> want to tend to...right there in the next room...calling
> my name. Obviously, I am not some sort of "working-
> world-meth-addict" on the verge of losing my marriage,
> friends, and family. I'm just saying that it is a challenge
> to walk away each night. The traditional office usually
> provides that time boundary for you. Self-motivated
> types should consider themselves warned.

I agree. I think the biggest challenge for most entrepreneurs is developing a schedule that creates a satisfying work-life balance — though I also think even self-identified "slackers" can change their ways and learn this. We live in an age where work finds you wherever and whenever. It is unavoidable, and yet that can also add healthy variety to a day of work. For instance, in pleasant weather, I work on an outdoor patio table with an excellent wireless connection.

A related issue is that, because working from a home office can be a lonely experience, it is important not to fall into the habit of hanging around in the office waiting for the phone to ring or for an email to arrive. I have always set myself a start time and finish time for the home-office environment. Otherwise burnout can occur easily. I start work at 9 AM and do that first task from my to-do list. At 10:30 AM, I schedule a half-hour break and take the dogs for a walk in the woods. This is as good as a power nap for me, and it refreshes my mentality. I like to work in ninety-minute segments, and I typically do the 11 AM to 12:30 PM slot at the desk. Lunch is also a ninety-minute break that includes a second walk or power nap (I use a hammock in the woods and get some great ideas there). I may return to the desk between 2 and 3:30 PM, but never beyond that. The rest of the day and evening I may occasionally check email and voicemail, but I never return to the desk.

I believe schedule discipline is vital to maintaining the success mentality. One thing you must never do is check email or texts just before going on your scheduled break because you will at the very least eat into your break time and at worst be sent on a lengthy business task that ends up eliminating the break. It takes practice and discipline to walk away, but success requires learning and maintaining new habits. Remember, most startups fail, and while some might have been run by "slackers," I guarantee that most were run by entrepreneurs who burned out by overworking all day every day while checking email constantly from the moment they got up to when they went to bed.

To help avoid the temptation to go into the office too early or stay too late, keep a pad and pen with you at all times, wherever you go. I have them beside my bed, in the kitchen, and on the coffee table in front of the TV. I carry them in my coat pockets and the car. When I get a thought or a reminder to do some task, or when an idea pops into my head, I write it down as soon as possible. This stops me from sneaking into the office "out of hours."

The Leadership Mentality

Good startup leaders are not born that way and do not have special access to any CEO-type secrets or talents. Everyone is equally capable of being successful.

There are, of course, dozens of books on the art and science of leadership, but for me leadership always comes down to one thing. If you can lead and direct a handful of people well, you can lead and direct anything. The style you use is almost irrelevant so long as the job gets done.

When I was a sales manager, I had seven sales representatives to lead. I don't know what they thought of me. As a national director, I was responsible for seven managers. I didn't care what any of them thought of me. As vice president, I led a team of seven department directors. I never asked for their feedback on my leadership style. As CEO of a virtual company, I hired and directed seven vendors. I will never know what opinions they had of me.

Regardless of the job or title, my main role was the leading of seven people. If you can lead a few people, then you have what it takes to be a successful leader of any size organization.

You don't need an MBA or some management course. You just need to be you, to be self-confident, and to have discipline. Whether you are a benevolent dictator or a cupcake is of no matter.

For instance, Google's CEO Larry Page has degrees in engineering and computer science. Richard Branson dropped out of school at age sixteen. Neither could be said to have been born leaders or to have some secret inside information on what it takes to lead well.

There is no single way to lead, and there is no common element among great leaders. Some are extroverts and some are introverts. Some are tall and some are small. Some have humor and some take themselves seriously. Some are conventional and others are not. Some experts say it is better to lead from behind and others say to lead from the front.

The short answer is that, when you put yourself in a position to lead, then you have to lead. People may judge you as a good leader or a bad leader depending on how they feel about you, but what does it matter? You don't have to get a good performance appraisal anymore. You own the company. The secret to leadership mentality freedom is to be independent of the *good* opinion of others. Just lead any way you feel comfortable. Ditch all those books on what it takes to lead, be yourself, and start leading. In the hub model, no one you work with needs to be told what to do. They just need to know in what direction they are going. Give others the big picture, then sit back and relax.

Balance in Leadership: Trust and Verify

The outsource business model for startups is a different dynamic than many are used to who come from a traditionally structured company. The vendors in a hub model (also frequently referred to as a model of alliances) often have years of expertise and already know what to do with your product or how to serve your business. That's why you hire them, and once you confirm vendors have the expertise you need, you have to trust them to follow through on your instructions and let them get on with their tasks.

In a traditionally structured workplace, however, no one trusts, and many entrepreneurs who come from large companies bring this attitude to their startups and become control freaks. They want to get involved in everything. For a vendor, this can be a real pain in the butt, and there is nothing more disruptive than for a new entrepreneur to tell an experienced vendor, "Well, that's not the way we did it in my previous company."

Of course, for a long time, management consultants and academics have touted the benefits of trust in the workplace, but in my experience, I have rarely seen it practiced in large companies. It is easy to understand why. In a traditional company, everyone wants to win the approval of their manager. And if we are responsible for someone else's work — like a re-port — we are unlikely to pass it up the chain without checking it thoroughly. That mentality goes all the way up the pyramid. Even the CEO needs the approval of his or her board of directors and investors.

Further, most employees are not empowered to make a decision without the consent of their boss, and they of their boss, and so on up the rungs of the corporate ladder. In one company I worked at, when the solution made it all the way to the CEO, he then referred it outside the company to an independent management consultant for verification. The whole system was one of second-guessing, which becomes a common trait of leadership. In your startup, however, there is no one to pass the buck to, and no one else to answer to. Trust yourself to make the right decisions, and trust your vendors to do their jobs without second-guessing.

Then balance this trust with reasonable and regular verification. Trust is essential, but being too trusting is as dangerous as not trusting at all. First, as I say earlier, select vendors and contractors carefully. Verify their expertise and their reputation; confirm that they offer the terms and relationship you want. Don't overdo this review process, but don't simply hire the first person or company that comes along. Oddly enough, I tend to fall into this latter category. I am sometimes too trusting and too hands-off.

Knowing your inclination is helpful. Confirm this by asking others (those you trust to be honest, of course) for their opinion. Lyn has always told me I can be too trusting, and this helps remind me to double-check my decisions. Sometimes, I have to push myself to be more hands-on than I would be otherwise.

According to a 2009 *Harvard Business Review* survey, people who trust too much and too readily tend to take an overly rosy view of others, assuming that most people are decent and would never harm them. They are more likely to indiscriminately share sensitive information about their company and less likely to do deep due diligence on the other party of a potential transaction. Their overly trusting behavior sets them up for potential grief later on. On the other hand, people who assume the worst about others invite grief right away.

In the *Harvard Business Review*, Roderick Kramer wrote:

> I have been grappling with this question for most of my thirty years as a social psychologist, exploring both the strengths and the weaknesses of trust. In the wake of the recent massive and pervasive abuses — and with evidence of more scandals surfacing each day — I

think it's worth taking another look at why we trust so readily, why we sometimes trust poorly, and what we can do about it....Human beings are naturally predisposed to trust — it's in our genes and our childhood learning — and by and large it's a survival mechanism that has served our species well. That said, our willingness to trust often gets us into trouble. Moreover, we sometimes have difficulty distinguishing trustworthy people from untrustworthy ones.

Another way to put this is: Trust is important, but so is good judgment. One tendency that skews our judgment is our inclination to see what we want to see. Psychologists call this *confirmation bias*. Because of it we pay more attention, and give more importance, to evidence supporting our beliefs, while downplaying or discounting discrepancies or evidence to the contrary. To forestall my own inclination to be overly optimistic, I like to double-check all my decisions, and I also ask every vendor for their honest opinion. At first, vendors say only what they think I want to hear because they want me to be a happy customer, but as we develop a relationship, they get more comfortable warning me if I am making a mess of something. Good leaders listen as well as talk.

In addition, researchers have identified a cognitive illusion that increases our propensity to trust too readily, too much, and for too long, which is the *illusion of personal invulnerability*. We tend to underestimate the likelihood that bad things will happen to us or to our business, which can lead us to overlook the negative signs that one of life's misfortunes is about to affect us.

Ultimately, I think we can find the appropriate balance between trust and verification in business by deepening our intuition. Take a break from work at regular intervals and give yourself time to reflect. Leave the office and go for a short walk when you get that gnawing feeling in the pit of your stomach. That may be nerves, or it may be a warning that something needs investigating.

The Customer Comes First Mentality

The customer comes first; the rest is just detail. Your customers are now your closest family. Their needs are more important than anyone's, including your own. When they speak, you shut up and listen. When they complain, you accept responsibility and improve. When they praise, you ensure everyone involved in their happiness hears about it. When they call, you answer or call back. When they need something, you help them, regardless of whether there is a benefit in it for you. You exist to provide benefits to customers.

Todd is a highly successful entrepreneur whom it has been my pleasure to know for the past fifteen years. We have worked on many projects together, and I hold him in the utmost regard. His customers adore him. It is not just because of his exceptional business skills, but because he goes out of his way to help them in any aspect of their lives. Whatever they need, he tries to find a solution simply because he cares.

I first met him while promoting a product at an exhibition. I listened in as he struck up a conversation with an attendee. As they talked, the woman expressed frustration that a key member of her staff had resigned. Todd thought he knew someone who would be a perfect replacement, but his contact details for her were out of date, and it had been several years since their paths had crossed.

He spent hours tracking her down. When he found her, he set up a meeting with the prospective employer, and it was a match made in heaven. Neither the employer nor the employee were ever customers for Todd, but over the years both referred dozens of people who became his customers.

Todd does not do things like this for any potential gain, but because they are the right things to do. It is his nature to put other people's needs first. That is why he is also a successful businessman. Todd treats everyone as if they were VP of purchasing at Walmart because, for all he knows, they might be.

Every time you communicate with someone, whether by letter, handshake, or voice, they are your number-one customer in that moment and must be treated as such. You have no way of knowing who they know, or who they work for, or the influence they have. Assume every customer is a friend of Bill Gates and treat them that way.

The Continuous Improvement Mentality

After World War II, American occupation forces in Japan brought in experts to help with the rebuilding of Japanese industry. One group was tasked with improving management skills, and they introduced a film to teach the three "J" programs (job instruction, job methods, and job relations). The film was titled "Improvement in Four Steps" (*Kaizen eno Yon Dankai*), thus the original introduction of *kaizen* to Japan.

During the 1950s, a culture of kaizen, or "continuous improvement," developed in Japanese manufacturing, and we can see the results of their success in the number of Japanese products in homes around the world today. Kaizen is synonymous with quality and with a desire across an organization, and in every employee, to suggest ways that systems and quality might be improved.

Many MBA-type courses fixate on kaizen as it applies to

the manufacturing process and largely miss the point of the philosophy. It is not about increasing production efficiency, although that is certainly part of it. It is about improvements in all aspects of a business, in every department, in every person, and in every system. It is about never resting on your laurels or feeling that you have arrived at some destination.

MBA courses also like to make kaizen mysterious and complicated by relating it to subjects like statistical analyses and quality circles. It is, however, a much simpler mentality: It is about always striving to do better tomorrow than you did today.

A culture of continuous improvement is essential for a successful small business, and it is the passion behind a virtual business model. By bolting on expert functions, each with their own desire to continuously improve their function expertise, you automatically become kaizen in nature. When selecting vendors, it is important to ascertain whether they also continually strive to improve, and one of the key questions I ask during the due diligence phase is about the vendor's future plans to improve the current systems they have in place. How do they monitor performance and what processes do they have for continuously improving?

As a startup entrepreneur, constantly ask yourself how you can improve in every aspect of your business. What small changes or updates can you make to your internet presence? How can you improve your sales information sheets? How can you improve your customer-service function? Is your auto-attendant greeting original and relevant? How cutting-edge is your accounting procedure? How can you improve your product to increase customer satisfaction? How can you improve your sales skills? How can you manage time better? How can you reduce costs and increase profit? This attitude should permeate every part of the business and be lived enthusiastically all the time.

The Fun Mentality

I hope this book has been a valuable guide to starting, surviving, and thriving in business. I hope I have demystified the concept of company ownership and shown that a little common sense and a few dollars can take you far without you ever leaving home, especially if you develop the disciplines to meditate and use your imagination. I wish you even more success than I have had, but I doubt anyone will be able to claim to have had more fun than me.

Life is not meant to be a struggle but a joyful process, and so is running your own business. I can think of few things as exhilarating as becoming your own boss for the first time and waking up with that sense of childlike excitement at the day ahead, a day that is as unpredictable as a child's game. Whatever your dream, please feel free to adopt my company mission, vision, and values statement:

- Make a positive difference in the lives of everyone involved,
- have fun doing it, and
- enjoy the material and other rewards of that endeavor.

The rest is just detail. I wish you every joy and happiness in building your dream. As Steve Jobs once advised:

> Your work is going to fill a large part of your life, and the only way to be truly satisfied is to do what you believe is great work. And the only way to do great work is to love what you do. If you haven't found it yet, keep looking. Don't settle. As with all matters of the heart, you'll know when you find it. And, like any great relationship, it just gets better and better as the years roll on. So keep looking until you find it. Don't settle.

The winner's path is not well traveled, and it can feel lonely at times. Fellow travelers and lots of helping hands can be found at www.trevorgblake.com, where I offer two support courses. "Transformation" develops creativity and mentality control and provides tools to help prepare you for success. I don't believe it is possible to have success until you are prepared for it, and there are ways to speed up that process.

"Company of 1" is a comprehensive guide to building the appropriate mentality of the single-person business in our new industrial age of automation. This is the best company structure to take advantage of what I believe is the opportunity of a lifetime: to achieve financial independence through your own venture, whether in commerce or the arts. Entrepreneurs need a new way of thinking and new tools to take advantage. Today, it is possible for anyone to work from anywhere and for less than five hours a day — in thirty years I have never worked more than five hours a day — and to achieve financial independence along with a balanced life of work, family, and relaxation. There will never be a better time to start your own venture.

Both courses include interaction with me, potential investors, and fellow entrepreneurs. You can also pitch your idea or sign up for a coaching and mentoring program. I donate profits from my programs to worthy causes, such as cancer research and development.

I look forward to hearing about all your adventures, most of which I am sure will be even more exciting than my own.

Endnotes

Introduction

p. xi   *Globally every year, more than 50 million people start new companies*: Moya K. Mason, "Worldwide Business Start-Ups," accessed August 20, 2019, http://www.moyak.com/papers /business-startups-entrepreneurs.html.

p. xii   *In 2017, 82 percent of new entrepreneurs were over forty years old*: The statistics in this paragraph come from the following sources: National Small Business Association, "2017 Year-End Economic Report," 2018, https://nsba.biz/wp-content/uploads /2018/02/year-end-economic-report-2017.pdf; American Express, "The 2018 State of Women-Owned Businesses Report," 2018, https://about.americanexpress.com/files/doc_library /file/2018-state-of-women-owned-businesses-report.pdf; and Matt Mansfield, "Startup Statistics — The Numbers You Need to Know," Small Business Trends, March 28, 2019,

https://smallbiztrends.com/2019/03/startup-statistics-small
-business.html.

p. xiii　*"Coping with ambiguity and surprises is more important than
foresight"*: Amar V. Bhidé, *The Origin and Evolution of New
Businesses* (New York: Oxford University Press, 2000).

Part I: Starting — The Global Pioneering Spirit

p. 3　*Every month in America, more than half a million people start
a company*: The statistics in this paragraph come from the following sources: "Kauffman Indicators of Entrepreneurship,"
accessed August 20, 2019, https://indicators.kauffman.org;
Louise Balle, "Information on Small Business Startups,"
Chron.com, accessed August 29, 2019, https://smallbusiness
.chron.com/information-small-business-startups-2491.html;
"Half of US Working Adults Own or Want to Own Their Own
Businesses, Finds University of Phoenix Survey," *UOPX News*,
August 4, 2014, https://www.phoenix.edu/news/releases/2014
/08/university-of-phoenix-survey-finds-half-of-adults-want
-own-business.html; and Mansfield, "Startup Statistics."

p. 4　*According to research, more than 50 million new businesses*: The
statistics in this paragraph come from the following sources:
Mason, "Worldwide Business Start-Ups"; American Express,
"2018 State of Women-Owned Businesses"; and NoCamels,
"Tel Aviv Among World's 'Heavyweight' Tech Hubs, Says New
Report," June 28, 2018, https://nocamels.com/2018/06/tel-aviv
-tech-hub-world.

p. 4　*In 2017, the United Kingdom reached over 600,000 startups for
the first time*: Andy Bounds, "Number of UK Start-Ups Rises
to New Record," *Financial Times*, October 12, 2017, https://
www.ft.com/content/cb56d86c-88d6-11e7-afd2-74b8ecd34d3b.

Chapter 1: Turn a Moment of Insight
into a Winning Idea

p. 8　*This made Branson mad, and he later said, "There is no point
in starting"*: Kieron Johnson, "Richard Branson: Your Business

Will Fail Unless You Know Your Customers and 'Experience Their Pain,'" *Business Insider*, November 29, 2017.

p. 8   *"I went to the back of the airport, hired a plane, borrowed a blackboard"*: Richard Branson, "Virgin Atlantic: 30 Years of Fun, Flying and Competition," *Telegraph*, June 21, 2014, https://www.telegraph.co.uk/finance/comment/10917094/virgin -atlantic-30-years-of-of-fun-flying-and-competition.html.

p. 9   *"I had misplaced the cassette," he admits. "It was all my fault"*: Reed Hastings, keynote speaker, California Charter Schools Association Conference, 2014, https://www.youtube.com /watch?v=ibmnllbviqu.

p. 10   *The story of Google's founding is another tale of success born of frustration*: The details and quotes about Google come from the following sources: Quora, "Google Wouldn't Exist without a Very Lucky First Break," *Quartz*, August 26, 2015, https://qz.com/489223/google-wouldnt-exist-without-a-very -lucky-first-break; and *The AUTM Briefing Book: 2015*, Association of University Technology Managers, 2015, https://www.cshl.edu/wp-content/uploads/2017/12/autm -briefing-book-2015.pdf.

p. 12   *It is also scientifically proven that writing by hand creates greater retention*: Lizette Borreli, "Why Using Pen and Paper, Not Laptops, Boosts Memory: Writing Notes Helps Recall Concepts, Ability to Understand," *Medical Daily*, February 6, 2014, http://www.medicaldaily.com/why-using-pen-and-paper -not-laptops-boosts-memory-writing-notes-helps-recall -concepts-ability-268770.

p. 14   *Steve Jobs believed intuition is "more powerful than intellect"*: EOC Institute, "The Ultimate Guide to Intuition & Meditation," accessed August 29, 2019, https://eocinstitute.org /meditation/develop-your-intuition-through-meditation.

p. 14   *In a 2016 study, only one-third of the CEOs surveyed said they trusted*: Melanie C. Nolen, "New Research Says CEOs Should Follow Their Intuition," *Chief Executive*, December 18, 2018, https://chiefexecutive.net/new-research-says-ceos-should -follow-their-intuition.

p. 15   *At Cornell University, Dr. Daryl Bem oversaw a decade-long series of experiments*: Daryl Bem, "Feeling the Future: Experimental Evidence for Anomalous Retroactive Influences on Cognition and Affect," *Journal of Personality and Social Psychology* 100, no. 3 (March 2011): 407–25, https://www.ncbi .nlm.nih.gov/pubmed/21280961.

p. 15   *one 2013 study concluded that women's abilities to make fair decisions*: Chris Bart and Gregory McQueen, "Why Women Make Better Directors," *International Journal of Business Governance and Ethics* 8, no. 1 (2013), https://pdfs.semanticscholar .org/a7db/04f990334daf8f0c47e587f61055b16518d0.pdf.

p. 16   *In 2016,* Forbes *said, "Today's corporate world may be male-dominated"*: Tonya McNeal-Weary, "Companies with Lots of Women Are Actually More Successful," *Forbes*, June 23, 2016, https://www.forbes.com/sites/tonyamcnealweary/2016 /06/23/companies-with-lots-of-women-are-actually-more -successful/#14fc07276e36.

p. 16   *According to University of Iowa researchers, the brain's so-called "axis of intuition"*: The studies in this paragraph come from: EOC Institute, "The Ultimate Guide to Intuition."

p. 17   *Fear is known to kill intuition*: Jessica Stillman, "Science: Your Anxiety Is Killing Your Intuition," *Inc.*, October 25, 2017, https://www.inc.com/jessica-stillman/science-stress-silences -your-gut-instincts.html.

p. 19   *In 2018, a* Scientific American *article described how distractions can actually be*: Cindi May, "The Inspiration Paradox: Your Best Creative Time Is Not When You Think," *Scientific American*, March 6, 2012, https://www.scientificamerican.com /article/your-best-creative-time-not-when-you-think.

p. 23   *"It is an experience of such perceptual vastness you literally have to reconfigure"*: Jason Silva, "Shots of Awe," YouTube, posted on May 22, 2013, https://www.youtube.com/watch?v=8qy vzrv3d3o.

p. 23   *According to one 2015 study, experiencing a sense of awe promotes altruism*: Paul K. Piff et al., "Awe, the Small Self, and Prosocial Behavior," *Journal of Personality and Social Psychology* 108, no. 6 (June 2015): 883–99, https://www.ncbi.nlm.nih .gov/pubmed/25984788.

p. 24   *Abraham Maslow, who wrote that these are "especially joyous"*:
         Abraham Maslow, *Religions: Values and Peak Experiences* (New
         York: Penguin, 1964/1970).

Chapter 2: Turn a Winning Idea into a Winning Company

p. 26   *in 2018, according to the Small Business Administration, 70
         percent of all businesses*: Mansfield, "Startup Statistics."

p. 27   *Psychologist Jerome Bruner said the "inhibitory system" of the
         RAS "routinely"*: This quote can be found in Eugene B. Shea,
         "The First Credible Theory of Cognitive Neuroscience?,"
         accessed August 20, 2019, http://www.howourbrainswork.com.

p. 39   *In 2017, according to the National Small Business Association*:
         National Small Business Association, "2017 Year-End Eco-
         nomic Report."

Chapter 3: Make That Company Real — Draft a Winning Business Plan

p. 45   *one study by* Inc. *magazine found that only 40 percent of the
         founders*: Sarah Bartlett, "Seat of the Pants," *Inc.*, October 15,
         2002, https://www.inc.com/magazine/20021015/24772.html.

p. 45   *A producer of business-plan software conducted a survey that
         found that those*: Rieva Lesonsky, "A Business Plan Doubles
         Your Chances for Success, Says a New Survey," Small Business
         Trends, January 20, 2016, http://smallbiztrends.com/2010/06
         /business-plan-success-twice-as-likely.html.

p. 47   *Dr. Lewis Terman, inventor of the Stanford-Binet IQ test, conducted
         a longitudinal*: For a description of this study, with links to the
         original research, see "Genetic Studies of Genius," Wikipedia,
         https://en.wikipedia.org/wiki/genetic_studies_of_genius.

p. 49   *"I started investing in startups in 1996"*: Peter Cohan, "The
         Anatomy of a Killer Business Plan," *Inc.*, August 7, 2012,
         https://www.inc.com/peter-cohan/the-anatomy-of-a-killer
         -business-plan.html.

p. 67   *The* Harvard Business Review *magazine regularly makes the
         point that to survive*: Matthew S. Olson, Derek van Bever, and

Seth Verry, "When Growth Stalls," *Harvard Business Review*, March 2008, https://hbr.org/2008/03/when-growth-stalls.

Part II: Surviving

p. 71   *it is well documented that among all companies, large or small, 82 percent fail*: Michael Flint, "Cash Flow: The Reason 82% of Small Businesses Fail," Preferred CFO, March 8, 2018, https://www.preferredcfo.com/cash-flow-reason-small -businesses-fail.

Chapter 4: Cash Flow Is King

p. 73   *the Small Business Administration states that new businesses have about a 40 percent*: Katie Horne, "Must-Read Small Business Statistics for Online Entrepreneurs in 2019," Digital.com, last updated September 24, 2019, https://digital.com/blog /small-business-statistics.

p. 79   *"Sales of its Osborne 1, a best seller in 1982, fell off sharply"*: The quotes in this story are from Harry McCracken, "Osborne!: The Machine, the Man, and the Dawn of the Portable Computing Revolution," *Technologizer*, April 1, 2011, https://www .technologizer.com/2011/04/01/osborne-computer/3. For more details on Osborne, see Fred R. Bleakley, "Behind the Big Collapse at Osborne," *New York Times*, November 6, 1983, https://www.nytimes.com/1983/11/06/business/behind-the -big-collapse-at-osborne.html.

p. 85   *"[Bezos] invited me to join Amazon.com Inc., which I did. But what I remember"*: Glenn Fleishman, "The True Story of the Amazon Door-Desk," Glenn Fleishman Writes Words about Things (blog), October 16, 2011, https://glog.glennf.com/blog /2011/10/16/the_true_story_of_the_amazon_door-desk.

Chapter 5: Gather Capital and Pitch to Investors

p. 93   *In an* Inc. *survey, 41 percent of CEOs stated that they launched their businesses*: Ilan Mochari, "The Numbers Game," *Inc.*, October 15, 2002, https://www.inc.com/magazine/20021015 /24778.html.

p. 93   *In an article in* Business News Daily, *he said, "Have a plan to cover your expenses"*: Sammi Caramela, "Startup Costs: How Much Cash Will You Need?" *Business News Daily*, April 12, 2018, https://www.businessnewsdaily.com/5-small-business-start-up-costs-options.html.

p. 94   *On its website, the Small Business Administration has very useful (and free)*: US Small Business Administration, "Calculate Your Startup Costs," https://www.sba.gov/business-guide/plan-your-business/calculate-your-startup-costs.

p. 95   *In fiscal year 2016, however, business loans outstanding for less than $1 million*: US Small Business Administration, "Small Business Lending in the United States, 2016," accessed August 29, 2019, https://www.sba.gov/advocacy/small-business-lending-united-states-2016.

p. 95   *In their surveys, the National Federation of Independent Business reports*: William C. Dunkelberg and Holly Wade, "NFIB Small Business Economic Trends," National Federation of Independent Business, January 2011, https://www.nfib.com/portals/0/pdf/sbet/sbet201101.pdf.

p. 96   *According to Northwestern Mutual's 2018* Planning & Progress Study: Northwestern Mutual, *Planning & Progress Study 2018*, accessed August 29, 2019, https://news.northwesternmutual.com/planning-and-progress-2018.

p. 102 *In April 1976, Apple was founded by three people: by Steve Jobs*: The details for Apple's story come from the following sources: Christoph Dernbach, "How the Founders of Apple Got Rich," Mac History (blog), accessed August 20, 2019, https://www.mac-history.net/top/2015-01-30/how-the-founders-of-apple-got-rich; Emmie Martin, "Apple Just Hit a $1 Trillion Market Cap," CNBC.com, August 2, 2018, https://www.cnbc.com/2018/08/02/why-ronald-wayne-sold-his-10-percent-stake-in-apple-for-800-dollars.html; and Darren Weaver and Will Wei, "Meet the Forgotten Co-founder of Apple Who Once Owned 10% of the Company," *Business Insider*, September 11, 2017, https://www.businessinsider.com/ronald-wayne-third-founder-apple-computer-2017-2.

p. 118 *This is difficult to describe in words, but there are excellent short videos*: For examples of body language in public speaking, see Julian Treasure, "How to Speak so That People Want to Listen," YouTube, posted June 27, 2014, https://www.youtube .com/watch?v=eiho2sozahi; Mark Robinson, "How to Present to Keep Your Audience's Attention," YouTube, posted August 4, 2016, https://www.youtube.com/watch?v=bmei zadvnwy; and Caroline Goyder, "The Surprising Secret to Speaking with Confidence," YouTube, posted November 25, 2014, https://www.youtube.com/watch?v=a2mr5xbjtxu.

Chapter 6: A Virtual Business — Build the Hub

p. 127   *meetings have increasingly become a great enemy to everyone in corporate America*: "$37 Billion Per Year in Unnecessary Meetings, What Is Your Share?" MeetingKing, October 21, 2013, https://meetingking.com/37-billion-per-year-unnecessary -meetings-share.

p. 132   *According to Professor Richard Foster from Yale University, the average life*: Kim Gittleson, "Can a Company Live Forever?" *BBC News*, January 19, 2012, https://www.bbc.com/news /business-16611040.

p. 133   *"In an early 2006 speech, [GM billionaire investor Kirk Kerkorian] spelled out"*: Sharon Silke Carly, "Seven Reasons GM Is Headed to Bankruptcy," *USA Today*, May 31, 2009, https://usa today30.usatoday.com/money/autos/2009-05-31-gm-mistakes -bankruptcy_n.htm.

p. 134   *One positive example is Amazon, which is the largest internet retailer*: For more on Amazon and virtual organizations, see Robert Bradt, "Virtual Organisations: A Simple Taxonomy," 1998, http://citeseerx.ist.psu.edu/viewdoc/download ?doi=10.1.1.202.88&rep=rep1&type=pdf.

p. 134   *Even large, previously inflexible companies such as IBM, Hewlett Packard, AT&T*: Marilyn M. Helms and Farhad M. E. Raiszadeh, "Virtual Offices: Understanding and Managing What You Cannot See," *Work Study* 51, no. 5 (September 2002): 240–47, https://doi.org/10.1108/00438020210437259.

p. 159   *A global study in 2015 by workplace provider Regus showed about a third*: Carol Toller, "The Unspoken Loneliness of Working from Home," *Canadian Business*, June 22, 2015,

https://www.canadianbusiness.com/innovation/the-unspoken
-loneliness-of-working-from-home.

p. 168   *A recent article in* Wired *questioned the long-term costs of*
          renting cloud services: Cade Metz, "Why Some Startups Say
          the Cloud Is a Waste of Money," *Wired*, August 15, 2013,
          http://www.wired.com/2013/08/memsql-and-amazon.

Chapter 7: Great Marketing and the Secret of Sales

p. 188   *In order to plan efficient TV media buys, 1960s advertising*
          expert Herbert Krugman: Herbert E. Krugman, "The Impact of
          Television Advertising: Learning without Involvement," *Public
          Opinion Quarterly* 29, no. 3 (fall 1965): 349–56, https://doi.org
          /10.1086/267335.

p. 189   *"Marketers see today's consumers as web-savvy, mobile-enabled*
          data sifters": Patrick Spenner and Karen Freeman, "To Keep
          Your Customers, Keep It Simple," *Harvard Business Review*,
          May 2012, https://hbr.org/2012/05/to-keep-your-customers
          -keep-it-simple#article-top.

p. 190   *The same* Harvard Business Review *article focused on what*
          makes consumers "sticky": Spenner and Freeman, "To Keep
          Your Customers."

p. 196   *A Gallup poll on the honesty of business professionals found*
          that insurance: Josh Voorhees, "The List of Who People Trust
          Less than Congressmen Is a Short One," *Slate*, December 3,
          2012, https://slate.com/news-and-politics/2012/12/gallup
          -trustworthy-poll-congressmen-car-salesman-least-trusted
          -professions.html.

Chapter 8: Winning Customers —
Build a Trustworthy Relationship

p. 213   *Harland Sanders was born on a small farm in Henryville, Indi-*
          ana: Ronald Shillingford, *History of the World's Greatest Entre-*
          preneurs (N.p.: The History of the World's Greatest, 2010).

p. 219   *recent studies have found that less than two-thirds of small*
          businesses have a website: Betsy McLeod, "60+ Small Business
          Statistics to Help Your Digital Marketing Strategy," Blue

Corona, October 2, 2018, https://www.bluecorona.com
/blog/29-small-business-digital-marketing-statistics.

p. 225   *In 2018, 47 percent of small-business owners spent less than
$10,000*: McLeod, "60+ Small Business Statistics."

Chapter 9: The Success Mentality

p. 232   *An excellent example is Circuit City, which Jim Collins wrote
about in his book*: Jim Collins, *Good to Great: Why Some Companies Make the Leap and Others Don't* (New York: Harper-
Collins, 2001).

p. 232   *"Circuit City was incredibly successful in the 1980s and 1990s"*:
Anita Hamilton, "Why Circuit City Busted, While Best Buy
Boomed," *Time*, November 11, 2008, http://content
.time.com/time/business/article/0,8599,1858079,00.html.

p. 234   *in a 2012* Forbes *article, the companies claimed the secret for
their success*: Carmine Gallo, "How Wegmans, Apple Store,
and Ritz-Carlton Win Loyal Customers," *Forbes*, December 11,
2012, http://www.forbes.com/sites/carminegallo/2012/12/11
/how-wegmans-apple-store-and-the-ritz-carlton-wins-loyal
-customers.

p. 237   *She wrote, "My lists keep me on track, and I give it all the
credit"*: Mary Kay Ash, *The Mary Kay Way* (Hoboken, NJ:
John Wiley & Sons, 2008).

p. 246   *According to a 2009* Harvard Business Review *survey, people
who trust*: Roderick M. Kramer, "Rethinking Trust," *Harvard
Business Review*, June 2009, https://hbr.org/2009/06/rethinking
-trust.

p. 251   *"Your work is going to fill a large part of your life, and the only
way"*: David M. Ewalt, "Steve Jobs's 2005 Stanford Com-
mencement Address," *Forbes*, October 5, 2011, https://www
.forbes.com/sites/davidewalt/2011/10/05/steve-jobs-2005
-stanford-commencement-address/#5caa820a5852.

Index

About the Author

Trevor Blake is the author of *Three Simple Steps*, a *New York Times* bestseller and a 2013 Small Business Book Award winner.

Trevor was founder and CEO of QOL Medical LLC, a company focused on solutions for rare pediatric diseases, which he started in 2002 with a few hundred dollars. Its virtual business model was unique in an industry crying out for change, and it sold in 2010 for more than $100 million. Using the same business model in 2006, he founded and served as CEO for ANU LLC to develop radio-sensitizing treatments for head and neck cancers. It sold in 2012 for an undisclosed fee to a Taiwan company. In 2012, he cofounded Neovia Oncology, a company developing first-in-class multitarget combination treatments for the most aggressive forms of cancer, and he serves as CEO.

Neovia has a unique portfolio of sixty-eight new chemical entities, with its lead compound in phase one, first-in-human clinical trials in the United States in 2019 for advanced solid tumors like colon cancer.

Trevor was previously VP of commercial development at Ceptyr (Seattle) and director of commercial development at Orphan Medical (Minnesota). He has worked in the United Kingdom, Europe, and the United States with companies such as Lipha, 3M, and Biogen, and he has won many industry awards, including pharmaceutical manager of the year in 1990, 1991, and 1992 and UK marketing professional of the year in 1993. In 1994 he transferred within his company to the United States and is now also a US citizen.

He is a graduate of Britannia Royal Naval College, and his first degree is BSc in radiation physics and nuclear medicine. In 1990, he also earned a master's in business administration from Durham University (UK), specializing in international business.

Trevor attributes all these good things to lessons he learned from the two powerful women in his life: his mother, who passed in 1982, but not before introducing him to her favorite nurse, whom he has now been happily married to since 1984.

Trevor's passion is physics and how we can use an understanding of the relationship between energy and matter to achieve success in any aspect of business and life.

www.trevorgblake.com